MW00950604

2025

CROCK POT COOKBOOK

for Beginners

Mathildetru Lauruiridsen

2000 Days Super Easy and Delicious Slow Cooker Recipes Book for Every Home-Cooked Meals, from Breakfast to Desserts, Lunch and Dinner

Copyright© 2024 By Mathildetru Lauruiridsen

All rights reserved worldwide.

No part of this book may be reproduced or transmitted in any form or by any means, electronic or mechanical, including photo- copying, recording or by any information storage and retrieval system, without written permission from the publisher, except for the inclusion of brief quotations in a review.

Warning-Disclaimer

The purpose of this book is to educate and entertain. The author or publisher does not guarantee that anyone following the techniques, suggestions, tips, ideas, or strategies will become successful. The author and publisher shall have neither liability or responsibility to anyone with respect to any loss or damage caused, or alleged to be caused, directly or indirectly by the information contained in this book.

TABLE OF CONTENTS

INTRODUCTION

In today's fast-paced world, finding time to cook nutritious, flavorful, and satisfying meals is a constant challenge. Between hectic work schedules, family responsibilities, and personal endeavors, the art of home-cooked meals can sometimes feel out of reach. Fortunately, the Crock Pot, a trusted slow-cooking companion, has emerged as a beacon of culinary possibility, transforming how we approach cooking. This humble kitchen appliance has redefined convenience in the kitchen, allowing even the busiest individuals to prepare hearty, delicious meals without sacrificing precious time or quality.

The slow cooker, commonly known by its popular brand name Crock Pot, isn't just a tool; it's a game changer. With its low and steady heat, it brings out flavors in a way that traditional methods often can't match. The concept is simple yet revolutionary: add your ingredients, set the desired temperature, and walk away. Hours later, you'll be greeted with mouthwatering aromas and a fully cooked meal. What makes this form of cooking so special? Let's delve into the versatility, health benefits, and cultural impact of Crock Pot cuisine.

A Versatile Kitchen Companion

The magic of the Crock Pot lies in its versatility. From savory stews and tender roasts to creamy desserts and plant-based dishes, this slow cooker can handle a wide range of culinary tasks. Imagine waking up on a crisp autumn morning and setting a pot of spiced apple cider to simmer, or preparing a hearty beef stew before heading to work and coming home to a comforting, ready-to-eat dinner. The Crock Pot effortlessly transforms simple, inexpensive ingredients into sumptuous meals that rival the dishes served in upscale restaurants.

What sets the Crock Pot apart is its ability to accommodate different cooking styles and dietary preferences. Whether you're a meat lover, vegetarian, or someone following a specific diet plan like keto, paleo, or gluten-free, there are endless possibilities. One-pot pastas, curries, grain bowls, soups, and even bread are just a few examples of the dishes you can craft. The versatility of slow cooking encourages creativity, as you can experiment with flavors, spices, and techniques to create unique meals that reflect your taste and lifestyle.

Moreover, the Crock Pot is a blessing for meal planners and batch cookers. If you're trying to eat healthier or save money, preparing meals in advance is key. The Crock Pot makes it easy to cook large quantities that can be portioned and stored for later use. It's an efficient way to feed a family or prepare lunches and dinners for the week, all while minimizing food waste and reducing time spent in the kitchen.

The Health Benefits of Slow Cooking

In addition to its convenience, the Crock Pot offers numerous health benefits. Slow cooking preserves the nutrients in your ingredients better than high-heat cooking methods. Vegetables, for instance, retain more vitamins and minerals, and meats become tender and easier to digest. The gentle simmering process also allows for better flavor infusion, which means you can reduce the need for excess salt or artificial flavorings. The result? Nutritious meals that are naturally delicious.

One of the standout features of Crock Pot cooking is the ability to prepare wholesome, balanced meals with minimal effort. By adding lean proteins, whole grains, and a colorful array of vegetables, you can easily create meals that meet your nutritional needs. For those looking to maintain a healthy lifestyle, the Crock Pot is a powerful ally. You can prepare healthy soups and stews that are low in fat but high in flavor, or you can experiment with global cuisines to make your diet more diverse and exciting.

The slow cooker is also ideal for making homemade stocks and broths, which serve as the foundation for countless healthy recipes. Instead of relying on store-bought options that often contain preservatives and sodium, you can create your own nutrient-rich bases. This simple step not only enhances the flavor of your dishes but also contributes to a healthier diet overall.

Saving Time Without Compromising Quality

For many, the greatest appeal of the Crock Pot is the time-saving aspect. Imagine starting a recipe in the morning before heading out for the day and returning home to a meal that's ready to serve. This hands-off approach gives you more time to focus on other important tasks or simply to relax and unwind. In a world where multitasking has become the norm, the Crock Pot offers a rare gift: the ability to prepare wholesome, home-cooked meals without being tethered to the kitchen.

Despite its convenience, the Crock Pot never sacrifices the quality of the meals it produces. Slow cooking tenderizes tougher cuts of meat and melds flavors in a way that conventional methods cannot replicate. The hours of simmering break down the natural fibers of food, resulting in dishes that are deeply flavorful and satisfyingly rich. What's more, the slow, even heat distribution ensures that your meals cook evenly, eliminating the risk of scorching or undercooking.

This combination of time efficiency and high-quality results makes the Crock Pot ideal for people with busy lifestyles, parents, students, and anyone who loves good food but has limited time to prepare it. It's a testament to the idea that delicious, home-cooked meals don't have to be time-consuming or complicated.

Embracing the Slow Cooking Culture

Beyond its practical benefits, the Crock Pot has become a cultural phenomenon, inspiring communities of home cooks to share their favorite recipes and tips. The resurgence of slow cooking has been driven by a collective desire to reconnect with the experience of creating nourishing meals. As our lives become increasingly digital and fast-paced, the act of preparing a meal in a Crock Pot symbolizes a return to simpler times—a way to slow down and savor life's little pleasures.

Social media platforms are filled with Crock Pot enthusiasts who exchange ideas, celebrate their successes, and encourage one another to try new recipes. From food blogs to cooking groups, the slow cooking community is thriving, offering endless inspiration and support for those embarking on their culinary journey. This book is a testament to that passion, showcasing recipes that are as diverse as they are delicious.

Whether you're a seasoned Crock Pot user or a newcomer looking to explore the wonders of slow cooking, this cookbook will guide you through an array of recipes that will nourish your body and soul. Each chapter is thoughtfully crafted to highlight the versatility and potential of the Crock Pot, helping you make the most of this incredible appliance. So, embrace the slow cooking revolution and discover the joys of meals made with care, patience, and love.

Chapter 1

Breakfasts

Chapter 1 Breakfasts

Bacon-and-Eggs Breakfast Casserole

Prep time: 15 minutes | Cook time: 5 to 6 hours | Serves 8

- 1 tablespoon bacon fat or extra-virgin olive oil
- 12 eggs
- 1 cup coconut milk
- 1 pound (454 g) bacon, chopped and cooked crisp
- ½ sweet onion, chopped
- 2 teaspoons minced garlic
- ¼ teaspoon freshly ground black pepper
- ⅛ teaspoon salt
- Pinch red pepper flakes

1. Begin by applying a thin layer of bacon fat or olive oil to the bottom of the crock pot.2. In a separate mixing bowl, combine the eggs, coconut milk, crumbled bacon, chopped onion, minced garlic, black pepper, salt, and red pepper flakes, whisking until well blended. Pour this egg mixture into the prepared crock pot.3. Place the lid on the crock pot and set it to cook on low heat for a duration of 5 to 6 hours.4. Once cooked, dish out the mixture while it's still warm and enjoy.

Maple Nut Harvest Granola

Prep time: 20 minutes | Cook time: 2 hours | Makes 5 to 6 cups

- ¾ cup extra-virgin olive oil, plus more for crock pot
- 4 cups old-fashioned rolled oats
- 1 cup raw shelled pistachios, almonds, walnuts, pecans, or hazelnuts, chopped if large
- ¼ cup packed brown sugar
- ½ teaspoon ground cinnamon
- ½ teaspoon coarse salt
- ½ cup pure maple syrup
- 1 tablespoon vanilla extract
- ½ cup dried apricots, dates, cherries, figs, raisins, blueberries, or cranberries, chopped if large

1. Brush the insert of a 5- to 6-quart crock pot with oil and preheat cooker. 2. Stir together oats, nuts, brown sugar, cinnamon, and ¼ teaspoon salt in the crock pot until well combined. Stir in oil, maple syrup, and vanilla, mixing until fully combined. Raise heat to high, partially cover, turning lid 45 degrees to allow moisture to escape, and cook on high, stirring every 30 minutes, until toasted and golden brown, about 2 hours (do not cook on low). After 1 hour, rotate cooker insert to prevent scorching. 3. Stir in dried fruit; then spread granola in a single layer on a rimmed baking sheet to cool completely. Sprinkle with remaining ¼ teaspoon salt, if desired. (Store in an airtight container at room temperature for up to 1 week.)

Slow-Cooked Blueberry French Toast

Prep time: 30 minutes | Cook time: 3 hours | Serves 12

- 8 eggs
- ½ cup plain yogurt
- ⅓ cup sour cream
- 1 teaspoon vanilla extract
- ½ teaspoon ground cinnamon
- 1 cup 2% milk

Blueberry Syrup:

- 1 cup sugar
- 2 tablespoons cornstarch
- 1 cup cold water

- ⅓ cup maple syrup
- 1 (1-pound / 454-g) loaf French bread, cubed
- 1½ cups fresh or frozen blueberries
- 12 ounces (340 g) cream cheese, cubed

- ¾ cup fresh or frozen blueberries, divided
- 1 tablespoon butter
- 1 tablespoon lemon juice

1. In a spacious mixing bowl, combine the eggs, yogurt, sour cream, vanilla extract, and cinnamon, whisking them together until smooth. Slowly incorporate the milk and maple syrup, continuing to whisk until everything is well combined.2. Layer half of the bread in a greased 5- or 6-quart crock pot, then top it with half of the blueberries, cream cheese, and the egg mixture. Repeat this layering process. Cover the crock pot and place it in the refrigerator overnight.3. Take the crock pot out of the refrigerator 30 minutes prior to cooking. Set it to low and cook for 3 to 4 hours, or until a knife inserted into the center comes out clean.4. To prepare the syrup, combine the sugar and cornstarch in a small saucepan. Gradually stir in water until the mixture is smooth. Add ¼ cup of blueberries and bring the mixture to a boil. Cook while stirring until the blueberries burst, which should take about 3 minutes. Remove the saucepan from heat and stir in the butter, lemon juice, and the remaining blueberries. Serve the warm syrup over the French toast.

Dill & Salmon Bagel Strata

Prep time: 20 minutes | Cook time: 4½ hours | Serves 6 to 8

6 large eggs	zest
1 cup whole or low-fat milk	½ teaspoon freshly ground white pepper
1 cup sour cream (low fat is okay), plus additional for serving	6 plain or egg bagels, cut into ½-inch pieces
3 cups cooked salmon in chunks	1 (8-ounce / 227-g) package cream cheese, cut into ½-inch cubes
¼ cup chopped fresh dill	½ cup drained and chopped capers for serving
¼ cup finely chopped red onion	
2 teaspoons grated lemon	Lemon wedges for serving

1. Coat the insert of a 5- to 7-quart crock pot with nonstick cooking spray or line the insert with a slow-cooker liner according the manufacturer's directions. 2. Whisk together the eggs, milk, and sour cream in a large mixing bowl until smooth. Fold in the salmon, dill, onion, lemon zest, and pepper. Add the bagel pieces and mix, saturating the bread. 3. Transfer half the mixture to the crock pot and dot with half the cream cheese cubes. Repeat the layers. Cover and cook on low for 4 hours, until the strata is cooked through (170ºF / 77ºC on an instant-read thermometer). Remove the lid and cook for an additional 30 minutes. 4. Serve the strata from the cooker set on warm with the additional sour cream, capers, and the lemon wedges on the side.

Egg–Potato Bake

Prep time: 20 minutes | Cook time: 6 hours | Serves 2

2 slices bacon, chopped	1 cup shredded Havarti cheese
1 cup pork sausage	½ cup shredded Colby cheese
1 onion, chopped	
1 cup sliced button mushrooms	5 eggs, beaten
2 garlic cloves, minced	1 cup milk
1 orange bell pepper, chopped	½ teaspoon salt
	½ teaspoon dried thyme leaves
Nonstick cooking spray	
3 russet potatoes, peeled and sliced	⅛ teaspoon freshly ground black pepper

1. In a medium skillet set over medium heat, cook the bacon and sausage until the bacon turns crispy and the sausage is nicely browned, which should take about 10 minutes, stirring occasionally. Once done, transfer the bacon and sausage to a plate lined with paper towels to absorb excess grease. Discard all but 1 tablespoon of the drippings from the skillet.2. Using the same skillet, still on medium heat, sauté the onion, mushrooms, and garlic in the remaining drippings until they become tender, roughly 5 minutes. Remove from heat and mix in the bell pepper, bacon, and sausage.3. Prepare the crock pot by lining it with heavy-duty foil and spraying the foil with nonstick cooking spray.4. In the crock pot, create layers starting with the potatoes, followed by the bacon mixture, and then the cheeses.5. In a separate medium bowl, whisk together the eggs, milk, salt, thyme, and pepper until well combined. Pour this egg mixture evenly over the layers in the crock pot.6. Cover the crock pot and cook on low for 6 hours, or until the internal temperature reaches 160ºF (71ºC) when checked with a food thermometer.7. After cooking, carefully use the foil to lift the dish from the crock pot, cut it into squares, and serve warm.

Slow-Cooked Fruited Oatmeal with Nuts

Prep time: 15 minutes | Cook time: 6 hours | Serves 6

3 cups water	spice
2 cups old-fashioned oats	1 teaspoon ground cinnamon
2 cups chopped apples	6 tablespoons chopped almonds, toasted
1 cup dried cranberries	
1 cup fat-free milk	6 tablespoons chopped pecans, toasted
2 teaspoons butter, melted	
1 teaspoon pumpkin pie	Additional fat-free milk

1. In a 3-quart crock pot that has been coated with cooking spray, mix together the first eight ingredients thoroughly. Cover the pot and set it to cook on low for 6 to 8 hours, or until the liquid has been fully absorbed.2. Once cooked, scoop the oatmeal into serving bowls. Top each bowl with a sprinkle of almonds and pecans, and add a drizzle of extra milk if you prefer.

Warm Cinnamon-Spiced Apple Delight

Prep time: 15 minutes | Cook time: 8 to 10 hours | Serves 8

10 apples, peeled and sliced	1 tablespoon ground cinnamon
½ to 1 cup sugar	
	¼ teaspoon ground nutmeg

1. Combine ingredients in crock pot. 2. Cover. Cook on low 8 to 10 hours.

Nutty "Oatmeal"

Prep time: 10 minutes | Cook time: 8 hours | Serves 6

- 1 tablespoon coconut oil
- 1 cup coconut milk
- 1 cup unsweetened shredded coconut
- ½ cup chopped pecans
- ½ cup sliced almonds
- ¼ cup granulated erythritol
- 1 avocado, diced
- 2 ounces (57 g) protein powder
- 1 teaspoon ground cinnamon
- ¼ teaspoon ground nutmeg
- ½ cup blueberries, for garnish

1. Begin by applying a thin layer of coconut oil to the inside of the slow cooker.2. Add the coconut milk, shredded coconut, chopped pecans, almonds, erythritol, avocado, protein powder, cinnamon, and nutmeg into the crock pot, mixing everything well.3. Cover the slow cooker and set it to cook on low for 8 hours.4. Once the cooking time is complete, stir the mixture to achieve your preferred consistency.5. Serve the dish topped with fresh blueberries for an added burst of flavor.

Creamy Cornmeal Porridge

Prep time: 10 minutes | Cook time: 4 to 6 hours | Serves 15 to 18

- 2 cups cornmeal
- 2 teaspoons salt
- 2 cups cold water
- 6 cups hot water

1. Combine cornmeal, salt, and cold water. 2. Stir in hot water. Pour into greased crock pot. 3. Cover. Cook on high 1 hour, then stir again and cook on low 3 to 4 hours or cook on low 5 to 6 hours, stirring once every hour during the first 2 hours. 4. Serve hot.

Nutty Oatmeal

Prep time: 10 minutes | Cook time: 7 hours | Makes 7 cups

- 1 cup chopped walnuts
- Nonstick cooking spray
- 2 cups rolled oats (not instant or quick cooking)
- 1 cup raisins
- 3 cups almond milk
- 1½ cups apple juice
- ⅓ cup honey
- ⅓ cup brown sugar
- ½ teaspoon ground cinnamon
- ¼ teaspoon ground nutmeg
- ¼ teaspoon salt

1. In a small saucepan over medium-low heat, toast the walnuts, stirring frequently until they become fragrant, which should take

about 2 minutes.2. Lightly coat the inside of the crock pot with nonstick cooking spray.3. In the crock pot, mix together the toasted walnuts, oats, and raisins until evenly distributed.4. In a large bowl, whisk together the almond milk, apple juice, honey, brown sugar, cinnamon, nutmeg, and salt until well combined. Pour this mixture into the crock pot over the oat mixture.5. Cover the crock pot and set it to cook on low for 7 hours, or until the oatmeal is thickened and tender. Serve warm and enjoy.

Overnight Apple Cinnamon Oatmeal

Prep time: 15 minutes | Cook time: 8 to 9 hours | Serves 7 to 8

- 2 cups dry rolled oats
- 4 cups water
- 1 large apple, peeled and chopped
- 1 cup raisins
- 1 teaspoon cinnamon
- 1 to 2 tablespoons orange zest

1. Combine all ingredients in your crock pot. 2. Cover and cook on low 8 to 9 hours. 3. Serve topped with brown sugar, if you wish, and milk.

Savory Ham and Gruyère Strata

Prep time: 10 minutes | Cook time: 4½ hours | Serves 8

- 8 large eggs
- 2 cups whole or low-fat milk
- 6 shakes Tabasco sauce
- 1 tablespoon Dijon mustard
- 8 cups torn soft-crusted French bread (if the crust is crispy, remove it and use the
- center of the bread)
- 8 ounces (227 g) sliced Black Forest ham, cut into matchsticks
- 3 cups shredded Gruyère cheese
- 4 tablespoons (½ stick) unsalted butter, melted

1. Coat the insert of a 5- to 7-quart crock pot with nonstick cooking spray or line the insert with a slow-cooker liner according the manufacturer's directions. 2. Whisk together the eggs, milk, Tabasco, and mustard in a large bowl until blended. Add the bread and ham to the bowl and stir to saturate the bread and distribute the ham. 3. Spoon half the bread mixture into the crock pot and sprinkle with half the cheese. Repeat the layers and drizzle with the melted butter. 4. Cover and cook on low for 4 hours, until the strata is cooked through (170ºF / 77ºC on an instant-read thermometer). Remove the lid and cook for an additional 30 minutes. 5. Serve the strata from the cooker set on warm.

Veggie Hash with Eggs

Prep time: 20 minutes | Cook time: 6¼ hours | Serves 2

- Nonstick cooking spray
- 1 onion, chopped
- 2 garlic cloves, minced
- 1 red bell pepper, chopped
- 1 yellow summer squash, chopped
- 2 carrots, chopped
- 2 Yukon Gold potatoes, peeled and chopped
- 2 large tomatoes, seeded and
- chopped
- ¼ cup vegetable broth
- ½ teaspoon salt
- ⅛ teaspoon freshly ground black pepper
- ½ teaspoon dried thyme leaves
- 3 or 4 eggs
- ½ teaspoon ground sweet paprika

1. Begin by applying a generous layer of nonstick cooking spray to the interior of the crock pot to prevent sticking.2. In the crock pot, mix together all the ingredients, leaving out the eggs and paprika, ensuring everything is well combined.3. Place the lid on the crock pot and allow it to cook on low heat for a total of 6 hours.4. Once the cooking time is complete, remove the lid and create a small well in the vegetable mixture for each egg. Carefully crack an egg into a small bowl and gently pour it into one of the wells. Repeat this step for each remaining egg, and then dust the entire mixture with paprika.5. Cover the crock pot once more and continue cooking on low for another 10 to 15 minutes, or until the eggs are cooked to your liking. Serve hot and savor the flavors.

Cheesy Basic Strata: A Hearty Breakfast Bake

Prep time: 10 minutes | Cook time: 4½ hours | Serves 8 to 10

- 8 cups torn or cubed (1-inch) stale bread, tough crusts removed
- 3½ to 4 cups shredded cheese
- 10 large eggs
- 3 cups milk
- 1½ teaspoons salt
- ½ teaspoon hot sauce

1. Coat the insert of a 5- to 7-quart crock pot with nonstick cooking spray or line it with a slow-cooker liner according to the manufacturer's directions. 2. Spread a layer of the bread into the crock pot and sprinkle with some of the cheese. Continue layering the bread and cheese until it has all been used, saving some cheese for the top. 3. Whisk together the eggs, milk, salt, and hot sauce in a large bowl. Pour the mixture over the cheese and bread and push it down to make sure the bread becomes saturated. Sprinkle the remaining cheese over the top. 4. Cover and cook on low for 4 hours, until the strata is cooked through (170ºF / 77ºC on an instant-read thermometer). Remove the lid and cook for an additional 30 minutes. 5. Serve the strata from the cooker set on warm.

Breakfast Hominy

Prep time: 5 minutes | Cook time: 8 hours | Serves 5

- 1 cup dry cracked hominy
- 1 teaspoon salt
- Black pepper (optional)
- 3 cups water
- 2 tablespoons butter

1. In a greased crock pot, combine all ingredients thoroughly, mixing until well blended.2. Cover the crock pot and set it to cook on low for 8 hours, or let it cook overnight for convenience.3. Once done, serve the dish warm as a delightful breakfast option.

Three-Cheese Vegetable Strata: A Savory Breakfast Delight

Prep time: 20 minutes | Cook time: 6 hours | Serves 2

- 1 tablespoon extra-virgin olive oil
- 1 tablespoon butter
- 1 onion, chopped
- 2 garlic cloves, minced
- 1½ cups baby spinach leaves
- 1 red bell pepper, chopped
- 1 large tomato, seeded and chopped
- 1 cup cubed ham
- Nonstick cooking spray
- 5 eggs, beaten
- 1 cup milk
- ½ teaspoon salt
- ½ teaspoon dried thyme leaves
- ⅛ teaspoon freshly ground black pepper
- 6 slices French bread, cubed
- 1 cup shredded Cheddar cheese
- ½ cup shredded Swiss cheese
- ¼ cup grated Parmesan cheese

1. In a medium saucepan over medium heat, heat the olive oil and butter. Add the onion and garlic, and sauté, stirring, until tender, about 6 minutes. 2. Add the spinach and cook until wilted, about 5 minutes. Remove from the heat and add the bell pepper, tomato, and ham. 3. Line the crock pot with heavy-duty foil and spray with the nonstick cooking spray. 4. In a medium bowl, beat the eggs, milk, salt, thyme, and black pepper well. 5. In the crock pot, layer half of the French bread. Top with half of the vegetable and ham mixture, and sprinkle with half of the Cheddar and Swiss cheeses. Repeat the layers. 6. Pour the egg mixture over everything, and sprinkle with the Parmesan cheese. 7. Cover and cook on low for 6 hours, or until the temperature registers 160ºF (71ºC) on a food thermometer and the mixture is set. 8. Using the foil sling, remove from the crock pot, and serve.

Spiced Pumpkin Cream Pudding

Prep time: 15 minutes | Cook time: 6 to 7 hours | Serves 8

- ¼ cup melted butter, divided
- 2½ cups canned pumpkin purée
- 2 cups coconut milk
- 4 eggs
- 1 tablespoon pure vanilla extract
- 1 cup almond flour
- ½ cup granulated erythritol
- 2 ounces (57 g) protein powder
- 1 teaspoon baking powder
- 1 teaspoon ground cinnamon
- ¼ teaspoon ground nutmeg
- Pinch ground cloves

1. Lightly grease the insert of the crock pot with 1 tablespoon of the butter. 2. In a large bowl, whisk together the remaining butter, pumpkin, coconut milk, eggs, and vanilla until well blended. 3. In a small bowl, stir together the almond flour, erythritol, protein powder, baking powder, cinnamon, nutmeg, and cloves. 4. Add the dry ingredients to the wet ingredients and stir to combine. 5. Pour the mixture into the insert. 6. Cover and cook on low for 6 to 7 hours. 7. Serve warm.

Cheesy Sausage and Mushroom Quiche

Prep time: 20 minutes | Cook time: 6 hours | Serves 2

- 8 ounces (227 g) pork sausage
- 1 onion, chopped
- 1 cup sliced mushrooms
- Nonstick baking spray containing flour
- 2 garlic cloves, minced
- 1 red bell pepper, chopped
- 1 cup shredded Cheddar cheese, divided
- 4 eggs, beaten
- 1 cup whole milk
- ½ cup all-purpose flour
- ½ teaspoon baking powder
- ½ teaspoon salt
- ½ teaspoon dried basil leaves
- ⅛ teaspoon freshly ground black pepper
- ⅓ cup grated Parmesan cheese

1. In a medium saucepan over medium heat, cook the sausage with the onions, stirring to break up the meat, until the sausage is browned, about 10 minutes. Drain well and add the mushrooms; cook, stirring, until the mushrooms give up their liquid and the liquid evaporates, about 5 minutes. 2. Line the crock pot with heavy-duty foil. Spray the foil with the nonstick baking spray containing flour. 3. In the crock pot, layer the sausage mixture, garlic, and bell pepper. Top with ½ cup of Cheddar cheese. 4. In a medium bowl, beat the eggs, milk, flour, baking powder, salt, basil, and pepper. Pour the egg mixture into the crock pot and top

with the remaining ½ cup of Cheddar cheese. Sprinkle with the Parmesan cheese. 5. Cover and cook on low for 6 hours, or until the quiche registers 160°F (71°C) on a food thermometer, the edges are browned, and the center is set. 6. Remove from the crock pot and let stand for 5 minutes; cut into wedges and serve.

Crustless Wild Mushroom–Kale Quiche

Prep time: 10 minutes | Cook time: 5 to 6 hours | Serves 8

- 1 tablespoon extra-virgin olive oil
- 12 eggs
- 1 cup heavy (whipping) cream
- 1 tablespoon chopped fresh thyme
- 1 tablespoon chopped fresh chives
- ¼ teaspoon freshly ground black pepper
- ⅛ teaspoon salt
- 2 cups coarsely chopped wild mushrooms (shiitake, portobello, oyster, enoki)
- 1 cup chopped kale
- 1 cup shredded Swiss cheese

1. Start by applying a thin layer of olive oil to the inside of the crock pot. 2. In a medium bowl, combine the eggs, heavy cream, thyme, chives, black pepper, and salt, whisking them together until well blended. Fold in the mushrooms and kale until evenly distributed. Pour this mixture into the crock pot and sprinkle the cheese on top. 3. Cover the crock pot and set it to cook on low for 5 to 6 hours. 4. Once done, serve the dish warm for a delightful meal.

Overnight Oatmeal

Prep time: 5 minutes | Cook time: 3 to 10 hours | Serves 8

- 3¾ cups old-fashioned rolled oats
- 8 cups water
- ½ teaspoon salt
- 4 tablespoons (½ stick)
- unsalted butter, cut into small pieces
- 2 cups milk or cream, warmed, for serving
- ¼ cup cinnamon sugar for serving

1. Begin by coating the insert of a 5- to 7-quart crock pot with nonstick cooking spray, or alternatively, line it with a slow-cooker liner as per the manufacturer's instructions. 2. In the crock pot, mix together the oatmeal, water, and salt until well combined. Cover the pot and set it to cook on low for 8 to 10 hours, or on high for 3 to 4 hours, until the oats reach a creamy consistency. Stir in the butter until melted and fully incorporated. 3. Serve the oatmeal warm, accompanied by warmed milk and a sprinkle of cinnamon sugar for added flavor.

Blueberry Apple Waffle Topping

Prep time: 10 minutes | Cook time: 3 hours | Serves 10 to 12

- 1 quart natural applesauce, unsweetened
- 2 Granny Smith apples, unpeeled, cored, and sliced
- 1 pint fresh or frozen blueberries
- ½ tablespoon ground cinnamon
- ½ cup pure maple syrup
- 1 teaspoon almond flavoring
- ½ cup walnuts, chopped
- Nonfat cooking spray

1. In a crock pot that has been sprayed with nonfat cooking spray, mix together the applesauce, diced apples, and blueberries until well combined.2. Incorporate the cinnamon and maple syrup into the mixture, stirring gently to distribute.3. Cover the crock pot and set it to cook on low for 3 hours.4. Just before serving, stir in the almond flavoring and chopped walnuts for added texture and flavor.

Pumpkin-Pie Breakfast Bars

Prep time: 15 minutes | Cook time: 3 hours | Makes 8 bars

Crust:

- 5 tablespoons butter, softened, divided
- ¾ cup unsweetened shredded

Filling:

- 1 (28-ounce / 794-g) can pumpkin purée
- 1 cup heavy (whipping) cream
- 4 eggs
- 1 ounce (28 g) protein powder
- 1 teaspoon pure vanilla

- coconut
- ½ cup almond flour
- ¼ cup granulated erythritol

- extract
- 4 drops liquid stevia
- 1 teaspoon ground cinnamon
- ½ teaspoon ground ginger
- ¼ teaspoon ground nutmeg
- Pinch ground cloves
- Pinch salt

Prepare the Crust: 1. Begin by lightly greasing the bottom of the crock pot insert with 1 tablespoon of butter. 2. In a small bowl, combine the coconut, almond flour, erythritol, and the remaining butter, stirring until the mixture resembles coarse crumbs. 3. Press this crumb mixture evenly into the bottom of the insert to create a crust.

Prepare the Filling:

4. In a medium bowl, mix together the pumpkin puree, heavy cream, eggs, protein powder, vanilla extract, stevia, cinnamon, ginger, nutmeg, cloves, and salt until everything is thoroughly blended. 5. Pour the filling mixture evenly over the prepared crust. 6. Cover the crock pot and set it to cook on low for 3 hours. 7. After cooking, remove the lid and allow the dish to cool for 30 minutes.

Then transfer the insert to the refrigerator to chill completely for about 2 hours. 8. Once chilled, cut into squares and store them in a sealed container in the refrigerator for up to 5 days.

Classic Welsh Rarebit with Cheese and Beer

Prep time: 10 minutes | Cook time: 1½ to 2½ hours | Serves 6 to 8

- 1 (12-ounce / 340-g) can beer
- 1 tablespoon dry mustard
- 1 teaspoon Worcestershire sauce
- ½ teaspoon salt
- ⅛ teaspoon black or white pepper
- 1 pound (454 g) American

- cheese, cubed
- 1 pound (454 g) sharp Cheddar cheese, cubed
- English muffins or toast
- Tomato slices
- Bacon, cooked until crisp
- Fresh steamed asparagus spears

1. In crock pot, combine beer, mustard, 2. Worcestershire sauce, salt, and pepper. Cover and cook on high 1 to 2 hours, until mixture boils. 3. Add cheese, a little at a time, stirring constantly until all the cheese melts. 4. Heat on high 20 to 30 minutes with cover off, stirring frequently. 5. Serve hot over toasted English muffins or over toasted bread cut into triangles. Garnish with tomato slices, strips of crisp bacon and steamed asparagus spears.

Banana Bread Casserole: A Sweet and Savory Breakfast Treat

Prep time: 15 minutes | Cook time: 6 hours | Serves 2

- Nonstick cooking spray
- 6 slices banana bread, cubed
- 6 slices French bread, cubed
- 1 banana, sliced
- 4 slices bacon, cooked and crumbled
- ½ cup chopped pecans

- 4 eggs, beaten
- 1½ cups milk
- ⅓ cup sugar
- 2 tablespoons honey
- 1 teaspoon ground cinnamon
- 1 teaspoon vanilla
- ¼ teaspoon salt

1. Spray the crock pot with the nonstick cooking spray. 2. In the crock pot, layer the banana bread, French bread, banana, bacon, and pecans. 3. In a medium bowl, beat the eggs, milk, sugar, honey, cinnamon, vanilla, and salt. Pour the egg mixture into the crock pot. 4. Cover and cook on low for 6 hours, or until the temperature registers 160ºF (71ºC) on a food thermometer, and serve.

Nutty Keto Crunch Granola

Prep time: 10 minutes | Cook time: 3 to 4 hours | Serves 16

♦ ½ cup coconut oil, melted	coconut
♦ 2 teaspoons pure vanilla extract	♦ ½ cup hazelnuts
♦ 1 teaspoon maple extract	♦ ½ cup slivered almonds
♦ 1 cup chopped pecans	♦ ¼ cup granulated erythritol
♦ 1 cup sunflower seeds	♦ ½ teaspoon cinnamon
♦ 1 cup unsweetened shredded	♦ ¼ teaspoon ground nutmeg
	♦ ¼ teaspoon salt

1. Lightly grease the insert of the crock pot with 1 tablespoon of the coconut oil. 2. In a large bowl, whisk together the remaining coconut oil, vanilla, and maple extract. Add the pecans, sunflower seeds, coconut, hazelnuts, almonds, erythritol, cinnamon, nutmeg, and salt. Toss to coat the nuts and seeds. 3. Transfer the mixture to the insert. 4. Cover and cook on low for 3 to 4 hours, until the granola is crispy. 5. Transfer the granola to a baking sheet covered in parchment or foil to cool. 6. Store in a sealed container in the refrigerator for up to 2 weeks.

Classic Cinnamon Roll Bliss

Prep time: 20 minutes | Cook time: 1½ hours | Serves 10 to 12

Buns:

♦ 6 tablespoons unsalted butter, room temperature, plus more for brushing	plus more for work surface
	♦ 2 teaspoon coarse salt
♦ 1⅓ cups warm water (about 110ºF / 43ºC)	♦ ¾ cup granulated sugar
♦ 1 tablespoon active dry yeast	♦ ¼ cup plus 2 tablespoons packed brown sugar
♦ 2 tablespoons honey	♦ 1 tablespoon ground cinnamon
♦ 3½ cups all-purpose flour,	

Glaze:

♦ 3 cups confectioners' sugar	♦ 2 teaspoon vanilla extract
♦ Juice of ½ lemon	♦ ¼ cup plus 2 tablespoons milk

Make the Buns: 1. Brush the insert of a 5- to 6-quart crock pot with butter. Line bottom with parchment paper and brush paper with butter. 2. Combine the warm water, yeast, and honey in a bowl; let stand until foamy, about 5 minutes. Add flour and salt. With an electric mixer on low, mix until just combined. Increase speed to medium and mix for 5 minutes; let stand 10 minutes. Combine butter, both sugars, and cinnamon in a bowl; mix until smooth. 3.

Preheat the crock pot. Turn dough out onto a lightly floured work surface and roll into a rectangle, about 9 by 15 inches. Sprinkle dough evenly with cinnamon-sugar mixture. Starting from one long side, roll into a log, pinching seams to seal in filling. Slice log into 10 to 12 rounds, each about 1½ inches thick. 4. Arrange rolls, cut side down, in the cooker. Wrap lid tightly with a clean kitchen towel, gathering ends at top (to absorb condensation). Cover and cook on high until cooked through, 1½ hours (we prefer to bake these on high). After 1 hour, rotate cooker insert to prevent scorching. Turn out onto a wire rack to cool before serving. Make the Glaze: 5. With an electric mixer, whisk confectioners' sugar, lemon juice, and vanilla until smooth. Slowly add ¼ cup milk and beat on medium. Add more milk, a drop at a time up to 2 tablespoons, to reach desired consistency. Drizzle rolls with glaze just before serving.

Breakfast Prunes

Prep time: 10 minutes | Cook time: 8 to 10 hours | Serves 6

♦ 2 cups orange juice	♦ ¼ teaspoon ground nutmeg
♦ ¼ cup orange marmalade	♦ 1 cup water
♦ 1 teaspoon ground cinnamon	♦ 1 (12-ounce / 340-g) package pitted dried prunes
♦ ¼ teaspoon ground cloves	
	♦ 2 thin lemon slices

1. In a crock pot, mix together the orange juice, marmalade, cinnamon, cloves, nutmeg, and water until well blended. 2. Gently fold in the prunes and lemon slices, ensuring they are evenly distributed throughout the mixture. 3. Cover the crock pot and set it to cook on low for 8 to 10 hours, or let it cook overnight for convenience. 4. Serve the dish warm as a hearty breakfast option, or enjoy it warm or chilled as a delightful side dish later in the day.

Dulce de Leche: Creamy Caramel Delight for Cookies

Prep time: 5 minutes | Cook time: 2 hours | Makes 2½ cups

♦ 2 (14-ounce / 397-g) cans sweetened condensed milk	♦ Cookies, for serving

1. Place unopened cans of milk in crock pot. Fill cooker with warm water so that it comes above the cans by 1½ to 2 inches. 2. Cover cooker. Cook on high 2 hours. 3. Cool unopened cans. 4. When opened, the contents should be thick and spreadable. Use as a filling between 2 cookies.

Coconut Bliss Bread

Prep time: 10 minutes | Cook time: 3 to 4 hours | Makes 8 slices

- 1 tablespoon butter, softened
- 6 large eggs
- ½ cup coconut oil, melted
- 1 teaspoon pure vanilla extract
- ¼ teaspoon liquid stevia
- 1 cup almond flour
- ½ cup coconut flour
- 1 ounce (28 g) protein powder
- 1 teaspoon baking powder

1. Grease an 8-by-4-inch loaf pan with the butter. 2. In a medium bowl, whisk together the eggs, oil, vanilla, and stevia until well blended. 3. In a small bowl, stir together the almond flour, coconut flour, protein powder, and baking powder until mixed. 4. Add the dry ingredients to the wet ingredients and stir to combine. 5. Spoon the batter into the loaf pan and place the loaf pan on a rack in the crock pot. 6. Cover and cook on low for 3 to 4 hours, until a knife inserted in the center comes out clean. 7. Cool the bread in the loaf pan for 15 minutes. Then remove the bread from the pan and place onto a wire rack to cool completely. 8. Store in a sealed container in the refrigerator for up to 1 week.

Hot Wheat Berry Cereal

Prep time: 5 minutes | Cook time: 10 hours | Serves 4

- 1 cup wheat berries
- 5 cups water

1. Begin by rinsing and sorting the berries, then place them in the crock pot and cover with water. Let them soak for the entire day, or for about 8 hours.2. After soaking, cover the crock pot and set it to cook on low overnight, allowing for approximately 10 hours of cooking time.3. Once cooking is complete, drain any excess liquid if necessary, and the berries are ready to be served.

Polenta

Prep time: 10 minutes | Cook time:2 to 9 hours | Serves 8 to 10

- 4 tablespoons melted butter, divided
- ¼ teaspoon paprika
- 6 cups boiling water
- 2 cups dry cornmeal
- 2 teaspoons salt

1. Start by using 1 tablespoon of butter to lightly coat the interior of the crock pot. Sprinkle paprika evenly over the bottom and set the cooker to high heat.2. Carefully add the remaining ingredients to the crock pot in the specified order, including another tablespoon of butter. Mix everything thoroughly.3. Cover the crock pot and cook on high for 2 to 3 hours, or on low for 6 to 9 hours, stirring occasionally to ensure even cooking.4. Once cooked, pour the hot polenta into two loaf pans that have been lightly greased. Allow it to cool in the refrigerator for 8 hours or overnight to set.5. To serve, slice the chilled polenta into ¼-inch-thick pieces. In a large nonstick skillet, melt 2 tablespoons of butter, then add the slices and cook until golden brown. Flip to brown the other side as well.6. For a breakfast option, serve the slices with your preferred sweetener.

Overnight Apple Oatmeal

Prep time: 10 minutes | Cook time: 6 to 8 hours | Serves 4

- 2 cups skim or 2% milk
- 2 tablespoons honey, or ¼ cup brown sugar
- 1 tablespoon margarine
- ¼ teaspoon salt
- ½ teaspoon ground cinnamon
- 1 cup dry rolled oats
- 1 cup apples, chopped
- ½ cup raisins (optional)
- ¼ cup walnuts, chopped
- ½ cup fat-free half-and-half

1. Start by spraying the interior of the crock pot with nonfat cooking spray to prevent sticking.2. In a mixing bowl, combine all the ingredients, leaving out the half-and-half, and mix thoroughly. Pour this mixture into the crock pot.3. Cover the pot and set it to cook on low overnight, ideally for 6 to 8 hours, so it's ready to enjoy in the morning.4. Just before serving, stir in the half-and-half for a creamy finish.

Pumpkin-Pecan N'Oatmeal

Prep time: 10 minutes | Cook time: 8 hours | Serves 4

- 1 tablespoon coconut oil
- 3 cups cubed pumpkin, cut into 1-inch chunks
- 2 cups coconut milk
- ½ cup ground pecans
- 1 ounce (28 g) plain protein powder
- 2 tablespoons granulated erythritol
- 1 teaspoon maple extract
- ½ teaspoon ground nutmeg
- ¼ teaspoon ground cinnamon
- Pinch ground allspice

1. Begin by applying a thin layer of coconut oil to the inside of your slow cooker.2. Add the pumpkin puree, coconut milk, chopped pecans, protein powder, erythritol, maple extract, nutmeg, cinnamon, and allspice to the slow cooker insert, mixing everything together well.3. Cover the slow cooker and set it to cook on low for 8 hours.4. Once the cooking time is complete, stir the mixture or use a potato masher to achieve your desired consistency, then serve warm.

Sausage Breakfast Risotto

Prep time: 20 minutes | Cook time: 7 hours | Serves 2

- 8 ounces (227 g) pork sausage
- 1 onion, chopped
- 2 garlic cloves, minced
- Nonstick cooking spray
- 1 cup sliced cremini mushrooms
- 1 cup Arborio rice
- 3 cups chicken stock
- ½ cup milk
- ½ teaspoon salt
- ½ teaspoon dried marjoram leaves
- ⅛ teaspoon freshly ground black pepper
- ⅓ cup grated Parmesan cheese
- 1 tablespoon butter

1. In a medium saucepan set over medium heat, brown the sausage along with the onion and garlic, cooking for about 10 minutes and stirring frequently to crumble the meat. Once browned, drain any excess fat.2. Lightly coat the interior of the crock pot with nonstick cooking spray to prevent sticking.3. In the crock pot, combine the cooked sausage mixture with the mushrooms and rice. Pour in the stock, milk, salt, marjoram, and pepper, and stir everything together until well mixed.4. Cover the crock pot and set it to cook on low for 7 hours.5. After cooking, stir in the cheese and butter, allowing the mixture to sit for 5 minutes before serving.

Peachy Overnight French Toast

Prep time: 15 minutes | Cook time: 6 hours | Serves 2

- Nonstick cooking spray
- ½ cup brown sugar
- 3 tablespoons butter
- 1 tablespoon water
- 1 teaspoon vanilla
- 8 slices French bread
- 1½ cups peeled sliced
- peaches
- 4 eggs
- 1 cup milk
- ¼ cup granulated sugar
- ½ teaspoon ground cinnamon
- ¼ teaspoon salt
- ⅔ cup chopped pecans

1. Line the crock pot with heavy-duty foil, and spray with the nonstick cooking spray. 2. In a small saucepan over low heat, bring the brown sugar, butter, and water to a simmer. Simmer about 5 minutes, stirring, until the mixture forms a syrup. Remove from the heat and stir in the vanilla. 3. In the crock pot, layer in the bread and the peaches, drizzling each layer with some of the brown sugar syrup. 4. In a medium bowl, beat the eggs, milk, granulated sugar, cinnamon, and salt. Pour the egg mixture into the crock pot and sprinkle with the pecans. 5. Cover and cook on low for 6 hours, or until the temperature registers 160ºF (71ºC) on a food thermometer and the mixture is set. 6. Remove from the crock pot, slice, and serve.

Fruity Steel-Cut Oat Delight

Prep time: 10 minutes | Cook time: 7½ hours | Serves 2

- Nonstick cooking spray
- 1½ cups steel-cut oats
- ½ cup dried cranberries
- ½ cup golden raisins
- ½ cup chopped dried apricots
- 5 cups water
- 1 cup almond milk
- 3 tablespoons brown sugar
- 2 tablespoons honey
- ½ teaspoon salt
- 2 teaspoons vanilla

1. Spray the crock pot with the nonstick cooking spray. 2. In the crock pot, combine the oats, cranberries, raisins, and apricots, and stir. 3. Add the water, almond milk, brown sugar, honey, salt, and vanilla, and stir. 4. Cover and cook on low for 7½ hours, or until the oats are creamy, and serve.

Spanakopita Frittata

Prep time: 10 minutes | Cook time: 5 to 6 hours | Serves 8

- 1 tablespoon extra-virgin olive oil
- 12 eggs
- 1 cup heavy (whipping) cream
- 2 teaspoons minced garlic
- 2 cups chopped spinach
- ½ cup feta cheese
- Cherry tomatoes, halved, for garnish (optional)
- Yogurt, for garnish (optional)
- Parsley, for garnish (optional)

1. Start by applying a thin layer of olive oil to the inside of the crock pot to prevent sticking.2. In a medium bowl, whisk together the eggs, heavy cream, minced garlic, chopped spinach, and crumbled feta cheese until well combined. Pour this egg mixture into the prepared crock pot.3. Cover the crock pot and set it to cook on low for 5 to 6 hours.4. Once cooked, serve the dish warm, garnished with fresh tomatoes, a dollop of yogurt, and parsley if you like.

Breakfast Wassail

Prep time: 5 minutes | Cook time: 3 hours | Makes 4 quarts

- 1 (64-ounce / 1.8-kg) bottle cranberry juice
- 1 (32-ounce / 907-g) bottle apple juice
- 1 (12-ounce / 340-g) can frozen pineapple juice concentrate
- 1 (12-ounce / 340-g) can frozen lemonade concentrate
- 3 to 4 cinnamon sticks
- 1 quart water (optional)

1. In the crock pot, mix together all the ingredients, leaving out the water. If the mixture tastes too sweet for your liking, add water gradually until the desired sweetness is achieved. 2. Once combined, cover the crock pot and set it to cook on low for 3 hours.

Ranch-Style Egg Casserole

Prep time: 10 minutes | Cook time: 3 hours | Serves 8

- 1 tablespoon extra-virgin olive oil
- 10 eggs
- 1 cup heavy (whipping) cream
- 1 cup shredded Monterey Jack cheese, divided
- 1 cup prepared or homemade salsa
- 1 scallion, green and white parts, chopped
- 1 jalapeño pepper, chopped
- ½ teaspoon chili powder
- ½ teaspoon salt
- 1 avocado, chopped, for garnish
- 1 tablespoon chopped cilantro, for garnish

1. Lightly grease the insert of the crock pot with the olive oil. 2. In a large bowl, whisk together the eggs, heavy cream, ½ cup of the cheese, salsa, scallion, jalapeño, chili powder, and salt. Pour the mixture into the insert and sprinkle the top with the remaining ½ cup of cheese. 3. Cover and cook until the eggs are firm, about 3 hours on low. 4. Let the eggs cool slightly, then cut into wedges and serve garnished with avocado and cilantro.

Crock Pot Granola Mix

Prep time: 15 minutes | Cook time: 4 hours | Makes 8 cups

- Nonstick cooking spray
- 4 cups old-fashioned rolled oats
- 1 cup slivered almonds
- 1 cup coarsely chopped pecans
- 1 cup sunflower seeds
- 1 cup shredded coconut
- ⅓ cup butter or coconut oil
- 2 tablespoons safflower oil
- ½ cup honey
- ⅓ cup brown sugar
- 2 teaspoons vanilla
- 1 teaspoon ground cinnamon
- ½ teaspoon salt

1. Spray the crock pot with the nonstick cooking spray. 2. In the crock pot, combine the oats, almonds, pecans, sunflower seeds, and coconut. 3. In a medium saucepan over low heat, heat the butter, safflower oil, honey, brown sugar, vanilla, cinnamon, and salt until the butter melts, about 5 minutes. 4. Drizzle the butter mixture over the ingredients in the crock pot and stir to coat. 5. Cover, but leave the lid slightly ajar, and cook on low for 3 to 4 hours, stirring every hour if possible, until the mixture is golden brown. 6. Remove the granola to greased baking sheets and spread into an even layer. Let cool, and then break into pieces. Serve or store in an airtight container at room temperature.

Chapter 2

Beans and Grains

Chapter 2 Beans and Grains

Salsa Rice and Beans Delight

Prep time: 10 minutes | Cook time: 4 to 10 hours | Serves 6 to 8

- 2 (16-ounce / 454-g) cans black or navy beans, drained
- 1 (14-ounce / 397-g) chicken broth
- 1 cup long-grain white or
- brown rice, uncooked
- 1 quart salsa, your choice of heat
- 1 cup water
- ½ teaspoon garlic powder

1. Combine all ingredients in crock pot. Stir well. 2. Cover and cook on low 8 to 10 hours, or on high 4 hours.

Split Chickpeas with Turnips

Prep time: 10 minutes | Cook time: 4 to 7 hours | Serves 6

- 2 teaspoons cumin seeds, divided
- 1 teaspoon mustard seeds
- 1 teaspoon coriander seeds
- 1 tablespoon rapeseed oil
- 1½-inch piece cassia bark
- 4 small turnips, peeled and chopped
- 1 cup dried split chickpeas, washed
- 4 cups hot water
- 3 ripe tomatoes, chopped
- finely
- 1 or 2 fresh green chiles, chopped
- 1½-inch piece fresh ginger, grated
- 1 small onion, sliced
- 2 garlic cloves, sliced
- ½ teaspoon turmeric
- 1 teaspoon salt
- ½ teaspoon chili powder
- Handful fresh coriander leaves, chopped

1. Start by preheating the crock pot on the high setting.2. In a dry frying pan, combine 1 teaspoon of cumin seeds along with the mustard and coriander seeds. Roast them until they darken slightly and release a fragrant aroma. After roasting, crush the spices using a mortar and pestle or a spice grinder.3. Pour oil into the preheated crock pot and allow it to heat. Next, add the cassia bark and the remaining cumin seeds, cooking for a few moments to enhance the flavors.4. Add the turnips, split chickpeas, and water to the crock pot. Then incorporate the tomatoes, green chiles, ginger, onion, and garlic. Stir in the turmeric, salt, chili powder, and the crushed spices.5. Set the crock pot to cook on high for 4 hours or on low for 6 hours. If you prefer a thicker dhal, remove the lid and cook on high for an additional 30 minutes to 1 hour.6. Once everything is soft and fully cooked, mix in the chopped coriander leaves for added freshness.

Mediterranean Sausage and Rice Bake

Prep time: 10 minutes | Cook time: 2 to 5 hours | Serves 4

- ¼ cup olive oil, plus 1 tablespoon
- 1½ cups uncooked brown rice
- 1 large yellow onion, chopped
- 2 cloves garlic, minced
- ½ green bell pepper, chopped
- ¾ pound (340 g) bulk ground
- Italian sausage
- 4 cups tomato juice
- 1 teaspoon Worcestershire sauce
- ½ cup red wine of your choice
- ½ teaspoon cayenne pepper
- 1 teaspoon sea salt
- ¼ teaspoon black pepper

1. Heat ¼ cup of the olive oil over medium-high heat in a medium skillet. Add the brown rice and brown, tossing frequently, for 2 to 3 minutes. Remove the rice to a small bowl and set aside. 2. In same skillet, heat the remaining 1 tablespoon olive oil over medium-high heat. Add the onion and garlic and sauté for 1 or 2 minutes until fragrant. 3. Add the bell pepper. Cook for 2 or 3 minutes until the bell pepper has softened. Remove the vegetables to a small bowl and set aside. 4. Add the Italian sausage to the skillet. Cook over medium-high heat until just browned, about 4 minutes. Remove from the heat. 5. In a blender or food processor, purée one-half of the vegetable mix, which should now be just cool enough to handle, until just smooth. 6. To the crock pot, add the tomato juice, Worcestershire sauce, red wine, puréed vegetables, and cooked vegetables. Add browned rice. Add the browned Italian sausage. Sprinkle in the cayenne pepper, 1 teaspoon salt, and ¼ teaspoon pepper. 7. Cover and cook on high for 2 hours. Switch to low heat and continue cooking for 5 hours. 8. Season with additional salt and pepper, as needed. Serve hot.

Smoky Lentil Medley

Prep time: 5 minutes | Cook time: 6 to 8 hours | Serves 8

- 2 cups barbecue sauce
- 3½ cups water
- 1 pound (454 g) dry lentils
- 1 package vegetarian hot dogs, sliced

1. Combine all ingredients in crock pot. 2. Cover. Cook on low 6 to 8 hours.

"Famous" Baked Beans

Prep time: 20 minutes | Cook time: 3 to 6 hours | Serves 10

- 1 pound (454 g) ground beef
- ¼ cup minced onions
- 1 cup ketchup
- 4 (15-ounce / 425-g) cans pork and beans
- 1 cup brown sugar
- 2 tablespoons liquid smoke
- 1 tablespoon Worcestershire sauce

1. In a skillet, brown the beef and onions until cooked through. Once done, drain any excess fat. Transfer the meat and onions to the crock pot.2. Add the remaining ingredients to the crock pot, stirring well to combine everything evenly.3. Cover the crock pot and set it to cook on high for 3 hours, or on low for 5 to 6 hours, until fully cooked and flavors are melded.

Butternut Squash Risotto

Prep time: 10 minutes | Cook time: 2½ hours | Serves 4 to 6

- ½ cup (1 stick) unsalted butter
- 2 tablespoons olive oil
- ½ cup finely chopped shallots (about 4 medium)
- 2 cups diced peeled and seeded butternut squash
- 1½ cups Arborio or Carnaroli rice
- ¼ cup dry white wine or vermouth
- 4¼ cups chicken broth
- ½ cup freshly grated Parmigiano-Reggiano cheese

1. Begin by greasing the insert of a 5- to 7-quart crock pot with nonstick cooking spray, or line it with a slow-cooker liner following the manufacturer's guidelines.2. In a large saucepan over medium-high heat, combine ¼ cup of butter and the oil. Once hot, add the shallots and squash, sautéing until the shallots soften, which should take about 3 minutes. Stir in the rice, cooking it until it becomes opaque and well-coated with the butter. Pour in the wine and let it cook until the wine has evaporated.3. Transfer this mixture into the slow-cooker insert and stir in the broth. Cover the pot and set it to cook on high for 2½ hours, checking at the 2-hour mark to ensure that the broth hasn't evaporated. Once cooked, stir in the remaining ¼ cup of butter and ¼ cup of cheese.4. Serve the risotto immediately, with the remaining cheese offered on the side for added flavor.

Spinach-Stuffed Farro Delight

Prep time: 15 minutes | Cook time: 7 hours | Serves 2

- Nonstick cooking spray
- 1 leek, white part only, chopped
- 1 cup sliced cremini mushrooms
- 2 garlic cloves, minced
- 1½ cups farro, rinsed
- 3 cups vegetable broth
- ½ teaspoon dried marjoram leaves
- ½ teaspoon salt
- ⅛ teaspoon freshly ground black pepper
- 2 cups baby spinach leaves
- ⅓ cup grated Parmesan or Romano cheese

1. Spray the crock pot with the nonstick cooking spray. 2. In the crock pot, combine all the ingredients except the spinach and cheese, and stir. 3. Cover and cook on low for 6½ hours, or until the farro is almost tender. 4. Stir in the spinach, cover, and cook on low for about 30 minutes more, until the spinach is wilted and the farro is tender. 5. Stir in the cheese and serve.

Cheesy Grits Casserole

Prep time: 10 minutes | Cook time: 8 hours | Serves 8

- 1 cup stone-ground grits
- 4½ cups chicken broth
- 4 tablespoons (½ stick) unsalted butter, melted and slightly cooled
- 2 large eggs, beaten
- ½ cup heavy cream
- 2 cup finely shredded mild Cheddar cheese

1. Begin by applying nonstick cooking spray to the insert of the crock pot, or line it with a slow-cooker liner according to the manufacturer's instructions.2. In the slow-cooker insert, combine the grits, broth, and butter, stirring until well mixed. Cover the pot and set it to cook on low for 4 hours. After this time, stir in the eggs, cream, and cheese until fully incorporated. Cover again and continue cooking for an additional 4 hours, or until the grits are creamy and the cheese has melted completely.3. When ready to serve, keep the cooker set on warm and ladle out portions directly from it.

Kale with Chickpeas

Prep time: 10 minutes | Cook time: 4 to 6 hours | Serves 6

- 1 to 2 tablespoons rapeseed oil
- ½ teaspoon mustard seeds
- 1 teaspoon cumin seeds
- 1 large onion, diced
- 4 garlic cloves, crushed
- 4 plum tomatoes, finely chopped
- 1 heaped teaspoon coriander seeds, ground
- 1 fresh green chile, chopped
- 1 teaspoon chili powder
- 1 teaspoon turmeric
- 1 teaspoon salt
- 2 (16-ounce / 454-g) cans cooked chickpeas, drained and rinsed
- ¾ cup water
- 7 to 8 ounces (198 to 227 g) kale, chopped
- 1 fresh green chile, sliced, for garnish

1. Begin by heating the oil in a frying pan or directly in the crock pot if it has a sear setting. Once hot, add the mustard seeds followed by the cumin seeds, allowing them to pop and release their fragrant aroma.2. Incorporate the diced onion into the pan and cook, stirring frequently, for about 10 minutes. Then, add the minced garlic and sauté for a few more minutes before adding the tomatoes. Next, mix in the ground coriander seeds, green chile, chili powder, turmeric, and salt.3. Stir in the chickpeas and water, then cover the crock pot. Cook on low for 6 hours or on high for 4 hours, allowing the flavors to meld and the chickpeas to soften.4. After the initial cooking time, gradually add the chopped kale a handful at a time, stirring in between each addition. Let it cook for another 10 to 15 minutes until the kale is soft and tender.5. Finally, garnish the dish with sliced chile for an extra kick.

Fruited Wild Rice Pilaf

Prep time: 20 minutes | Cook time: 3½ to 7¾ hours | Serves 8 to 10

- 2 cups wild rice, rinsed with cold water and drained twice
- ½ cup (1 stick) unsalted butter
- 1 medium onion, finely chopped
- 3 stalks celery, finely chopped
- 1 teaspoon dried marjoram
- 4 to 5 cups chicken broth
- ½ cup finely chopped dried apricots
- ½ cup dried cranberries
- ½ teaspoon freshly ground black pepper
- ½ cup sliced almonds, toasted

1. Start by applying a layer of nonstick cooking spray to the insert of a 5- to 7-quart crock pot, or alternatively, line it with a slow-cooker liner according to the manufacturer's instructions.2. Add the rice to the slow-cooker insert. In a large skillet over medium-high heat, melt the butter. Once melted, add the onion, celery, and marjoram, sautéing until the vegetables have softened, which should take about 4 minutes.3. Transfer the sautéed vegetables into the slow-cooker insert. Then, mix in the broth, apricots, cranberries, and pepper. Cover the crock pot and set it to cook on high for 2½ to 3 hours, or on low for 7 hours, until the rice is tender. Be sure to check periodically to ensure there is enough liquid in the pot, adding more broth if necessary. After the rice is tender, uncover the crock pot and continue cooking on low for an additional 30 to 45 minutes. Finally, stir in the almonds.4. When ready to serve, keep the crock pot on low and serve directly from it.

Spicy Bean Medley

Prep time: 10 minutes | Cook time: 3 to 4 hours | Serves 8 to 10

- 1 (16-ounce / 454-g) can kidney beans, drained
- 1 (15-ounce / 425-g) can lima beans, drained
- ¼ cup vinegar
- 2 tablespoons molasses
- 2 heaping tablespoons brown sugar
- 2 tablespoons minced onion
- Mustard to taste
- Tabasco sauce to taste

1. Place beans in crock pot. 2. Combine remaining ingredients. Pour over beans. 3. Cover. Cook on low 3 to 4 hours.

Hearty Bean Medley

Prep time: 30 minutes | Cook time: 3 to 4 hours | Serves 15 to 20

- 8 bacon strips, diced
- 2 onions, thinly sliced
- 1 cup packed brown sugar
- ½ cup cider vinegar
- 1 teaspoon salt
- 1 teaspoon ground mustard
- ½ teaspoon garlic powder
- 1 (28-ounce / 794-g) can baked beans
- 1 (16-ounce / 454-g) can
- kidney beans, rinsed and drained
- 1 (15½-ounce / 439-g) can pinto beans, rinsed and drained
- 1 (15-ounce / 425-g) can lima beans, rinsed and drained
- 1 (15½-ounce / 439-g) can black-eyed peas, rinsed and drained

1. Cook bacon in skillet until crisp. Remove to paper towels. 2. Drain, reserving 2 tablespoons drippings. 3. Sauté onions in drippings until tender. 4. Add brown sugar, vinegar, salt, mustard, and garlic powder to skillet. Bring to boil. 5. Combine beans and peas in crock pot. Add onion mixture and bacon. Mix well. 6. Cover. Cook on high 3 to 4 hours.

Smoky Southern Lima Bean Medley

Prep time: 10 minutes | Cook time: 8 to 10 hours | Serves 6

♦ 1¼ cups dried lima beans	♦ 1 teaspoon cider vinegar
♦ Half a medium onion, chopped in large pieces	♦ 2 tablespoons molasses
♦ ½ teaspoon salt	♦ ¼ cup chili sauce or medium salsa
♦ ½ teaspoon dry mustard	♦ Several drops Tabasco sauce

1. Place beans in bowl and cover with water. Let beans soak overnight. Drain, reserving 1 cup liquid from beans. 2. Combine all ingredients in crock pot, including 1 cup bean liquid. 3. Cook on low 8 to 10 hours.

Easy Wheat Berries

Prep time: 10 minutes | Cook time: 2 hours | Serves 4 to 6

♦ 1 cup wheat berries	broth
♦ 1 cup couscous or small pasta like orzo	♦ ½ to 1 broth can of water
	♦ ½ cup dried raisins
♦ 1 (14½-ounce / 411-g) can	

1. Begin by soaking the wheat berries in water for 2 hours to ensure they soften, then drain the excess water. Place the soaked wheat berries into the slow cooker. 2. Add all other ingredients to the crock pot, mixing them together well to ensure even distribution. 3. Secure the lid on the slow cooker and cook on low heat for about 2 hours, or until the liquid has been absorbed and the wheat berries are tender.

Hometown Spanish Rice

Prep time: 20 minutes | Cook time: 2 to 4 hours | Serves 6 to 8

♦ 1 large onion, chopped	cooked
♦ 1 bell pepper, chopped	♦ 1 (28-ounce / 794-g) can stewed tomatoes with juice
♦ 1 pound (454 g) bacon, cooked, and broken into bite-size pieces	♦ Grated Parmesan cheese (optional)
♦ 2 cups long-grain rice,	♦ Nonstick cooking spray

1. In a small nonstick frying pan, sauté the onion and pepper until they are tender and fragrant. 2. Lightly spray the interior of the crock pot with nonstick cooking spray to prevent sticking. 3. In the crock pot, combine all the ingredients, including the sautéed onion and pepper. 4. Cover the crock pot and set it to cook on low for 4 hours, or on high for 2 hours, until everything is heated through. 5. If desired, sprinkle freshly grated Parmesan cheese on top just before serving for an extra layer of flavor.

White Beans with Kale

Prep time: 15 minutes | Cook time: 7½ hours | Serves 2

♦ 1 onion, chopped	♦ 2 cups vegetable broth
♦ 1 leek, white part only, sliced	♦ ½ teaspoon salt
♦ 2 celery stalks, sliced	♦ ½ teaspoon dried thyme leaves
♦ 2 garlic cloves, minced	♦ ⅛ teaspoon freshly ground black pepper
♦ 1 cup dried white lima beans or cannellini beans, sorted and rinsed	♦ 3 cups torn kale

1. In the crock pot, mix together all the ingredients, reserving the kale for later. 2. Cover the pot and set it to cook on low for 7 hours, or until the beans become tender. 3. Once the beans are cooked, add the kale to the mixture and stir well to combine. 4. Cover the pot again and switch the setting to high, cooking for an additional 30 minutes, or until the kale is tender yet still maintains a bit of firmness, then serve.

Tangy Three-Bean Delight

Prep time: 10 minutes | Cook time: 6 to 8 hours | Serves 8

♦ 4 slices lean bacon	♦ 1 (16-ounce / 454-g) can low-sodium lima beans, drained
♦ 1 onion, chopped	
♦ ¼ cup brown sugar	
♦ 1 teaspoon prepared mustard	♦ 1 (16-ounce / 454-g) can low-sodium baked beans, undrained
♦ 1 clove garlic, crushed	
♦ ½ teaspoon salt	♦ 1 (16-ounce / 454-g) can low-sodium kidney beans, drained
♦ ¼ cup vinegar	

1. Brown bacon in a nonstick skillet. Crumble. Combine bacon, 2 tablespoons drippings from bacon, onion, brown sugar, mustard, garlic, salt, and vinegar. 2. Mix with beans in crock pot. 3. Cover. Cook on low 6 to 8 hours.

Creamy Black Lentil Dhal

Prep time: 10 minutes | Cook time: 8 to 10 hours | Serves 6

- 2 cups dry whole black lentils
- 1 medium onion, finely chopped
- 1 heaped tablespoon freshly grated ginger
- 3 garlic cloves, chopped
- 3 fresh tomatoes, puréed, or 7 to 8 ounces (198 to 227 g) canned tomatoes, blended
- 2 fresh green chiles, chopped
- 2 tablespoons ghee
- ½ teaspoon turmeric

- 1 teaspoon chili powder
- 2 teaspoons coriander seeds, ground
- 1 teaspoon cumin seeds, ground
- 1 teaspoon sea salt
- 6⅓ cups water
- 1 to 2 tablespoons butter (optional)
- 1 teaspoon garam masala
- 1 teaspoon dried fenugreek leaves
- Handful fresh coriander leaves, chopped

1. Preheat the crock pot on high. 2. Clean and wash the black lentils. 3. Put the lentils, onion, ginger, garlic, tomatoes, chiles, ghee, turmeric, chili powder, coriander seeds, cumin seeds, salt, and water into the crock pot. Cover and cook for 10 hours on low or for 8 hours on high. 4. When the lentils are cooked and creamy, stir in the butter (if using), garam masala, and fenugreek leaves to make the dhal rich and delicious. Garnish with a sprinkle of fresh coriander leaves and serve.

Makes-A-Meal Baked Beans

Prep time: 15 minutes | Cook time: 3 hours | Serves 6 to 8

- 1 pound (454 g) ground beef
- ½ cup chopped onions
- ½ teaspoon taco seasoning, or more

- 1 or 2 (15-ounce / 425-g) cans pork and beans
- ¾ cup barbecue sauce

1. In a nonstick skillet, cook the ground beef and chopped onions over medium heat until browned, then drain any excess fat.2. In a slow cooker, combine the drained beef and onions with all the remaining ingredients, stirring well to mix everything thoroughly.3. Put the lid on the slow cooker and set it to low, letting it simmer for 3 hours until all flavors meld beautifully.

Savory Bean Combo

Prep time: 10 minutes | Cook time: 4 to 5 hours | Serves 6

- 1 (16-ounce / 454-g) can kidney beans, drained
- 1 (15½-ounce / 439-g) can baked beans, undrained
- 1 pint home-frozen, or 1 (1-pound / 454-g) package frozen, lima beans
- 1 pint home-frozen, or 1 (1-pound / 454-g) package frozen, green beans

- 4 slices lean turkey bacon, browned and crumbled
- ½ cup ketchup
- ⅓ cup sugar
- ⅓ cup brown sugar
- 2 tablespoons vinegar
- ½ teaspoon salt

1. Combine beans and bacon in crock pot. 2. Stir together remaining ingredients. Add to beans and mix well. 3. Cover. Cook on low 4 to 5 hours.

Chapter **3**

Poultry

Chapter 3 Poultry

Savory Italian Chicken Stew

Prep time: 15 minutes | Cook time: 6 hours | Serves 6

- 1 large onion, thinly sliced
- 3 pounds (1.4 kg) boneless, skinless chicken thighs
- 1 teaspoon kosher salt, plus more for seasoning
- 1 teaspoon freshly ground pepper, plus more for seasoning
- ½ cup all-purpose flour
- 2 (4½-ounce / 128-g) cans tomato paste
- 1 green bell pepper, seeded and finely chopped
- 4 ounces (113 g) fresh or canned mushrooms
- 3 tablespoons capers, drained and rinsed
- 4 garlic cloves, minced
- 3 teaspoons Italian seasoning
- 1 teaspoon red pepper flakes
- ½ cup dry white wine

1. Put the chicken in the crock pot, along with the onion, garlic, jalapeño, chili powder, cumin, salt, pepper, tomatoes, tomato paste, vinegar, Worcestershire sauce, hot sauce, and chicken stock. Stir to combine. Cover and cook on low for 8 hours. 2. Use two forks to shred the chicken inside the crock pot. Season with additional salt and pepper, as needed. Ladle the soup into bowls and garnish with your choice of tortilla chips, cilantro, sour cream, avocado, and a squirt of lime.

Chicken–Green Olive Stew

Prep time: 20 minutes | Cook time: 4 hours | Serves 4

- 1 (28-ounce / 794-g) can diced tomatoes, drained
- 1 cup chicken stock
- 1 large yellow onion, sliced
- 1 garlic clove, minced
- 1 teaspoon ground cumin
- 1 teaspoon paprika
- ½ teaspoon ground turmeric
- 1 tablespoon olive oil
- 1 (3-pound / 1.4-kg) skinless quartered chicken
- ½ teaspoon black pepper
- ¼ teaspoon sea salt
- ½ cup red wine
- ½ cup pitted green olives
- Zest of 1 lemon
- 2 cups hot cooked couscous
- ¼ cup sliced almonds, toasted

1. Add the tomatoes, stock, onion, and garlic to the slow cooker, then sprinkle in the cumin, paprika, and turmeric for flavor. 2. In a large skillet over medium-high heat, warm the olive oil, swirling it to coat the bottom of the pan. 3. Season the chicken with salt and pepper, then place it in the skillet. Sear the chicken for about 8 minutes, browning it on all sides before transferring it to the crock pot. 4. Pour the wine into the skillet, using a wooden spoon to scrape up the flavorful browned bits from the bottom of the pan. Add this mixture to the slow cooker. 5. Cover the slow cooker and cook on high for 4 hours. Thirty minutes before the cooking time is up, stir in the olives and lemon zest for added zest. 6. Once cooked, remove the chicken from the crock pot and let it cool on a plate. Shred the meat from the bones and return it to the crock pot, discarding the bones. 7. Serve the hot chicken stew over couscous and garnish with toasted almonds for a delightful crunch.

The Best Thanksgiving Turkey Breast You'll Ever Eat

Prep time: 20 minutes | Cook time: 3½ to 4 hours | Serves 8

- 2 medium onions, quartered
- 2 medium carrots, cut into 1-inch lengths
- 2 stalks celery, cut into 1-inch lengths
- 2 large sprigs thyme leaves
- 1½ teaspoons salt
- ½ teaspoon freshly ground
- black pepper
- 1 cup double-strength chicken broth
- 4 strips thick-cut bacon
- 1 (3- to 4-pound / 1.4- to 1.8-kg) bone-in turkey breast
- 2 teaspoons Wondra or other instant blending flour (optional)

1. Place the vegetables and thyme into the insert of a 5- to 7-quart slow cooker. Season with salt and pepper, then pour in the broth. 2. Lay the bacon over the turkey breast and set it in the slow cooker on top of the vegetables. Cover the cooker and set it to high, cooking for 3½ to 4 hours, or until the turkey breast reaches an internal temperature of 170ºF (77ºC) as measured with an instant-read thermometer. Carefully remove the turkey breast and place it on a serving platter, discarding the bacon. 3. Cover the turkey breast with aluminum foil and let it rest for 15 minutes. Meanwhile, strain the sauce through a fine-mesh sieve into a saucepan and bring it to a boil. If desired, whisk in the flour and allow it to reach a boil again. Taste the sauce and adjust the seasoning as necessary. Slice the turkey breast and serve it alongside the gravy.

Tangy BBQ Chicken Delight

Prep time: 10 minutes | Cook time: 3 to 8 hours | Serves 8

- 8 boneless, skinless chicken breast halves
- 1 (8-ounce / 227-g) can low-sodium tomato sauce
- 1 (8-ounce / 227-g) can water
- 2 tablespoons brown sugar
- 2 tablespoons prepared mustard
- 2 tablespoons Worcestershire sauce
- ¼ cup cider vinegar
- ½ teaspoon salt
- ¼ teaspoon black pepper
- Dash of garlic powder
- Dash of dried oregano
- 3 tablespoons onion, chopped
- Nonfat cooking spray

1. Place chicken in crock pot sprayed with nonfat cooking spray. Overlap chicken as little as possible. 2. Combine remaining ingredients. Pour over chicken. 3. Cover. Cook on low 6 to 8 hours, or on high 3 to 4 hours. 4. To thicken the sauce a bit, remove the lid during the last hour of cooking.

Old Delhi Butter Chicken

Prep time: 15 minutes | Cook time: 3 to 7 hours | Serves 6

Tomato Sauce:
- 3 medium red onions, roughly chopped
- 2 to 3 fresh green chiles
- 1 tablespoon freshly grated ginger
- 6 garlic cloves, roughly chopped
- 2¾-inch piece cassia bark
- 5 green cardamom pods
- 4 cloves
- 10 black peppercorns
Chicken:
- 2 tablespoons ghee or butter
- 1 tablespoon cumin seeds
- 12 chicken thighs, skinned, trimmed, and cut into cubes
- 1 to 2 tablespoons honey
- 1 tablespoon dried fenugreek
- 1 teaspoon salt
- 10 ripe red tomatoes, roughly chopped, or 1 (14-ounce / 397-g) can plum tomatoes
- 1 tablespoon tomato paste
- ½ teaspoon turmeric
- 1 tablespoon Kashmiri chili powder
- 2 teaspoons coriander seeds, ground
- 2 cups hot water
- leaves
- ⅓ cup heavy cream (optional)
- 1 tablespoon butter (optional)
- Coriander leaves to garnish (optional)

Prepare the Tomato Sauce: 1. Start by setting your slow cooker to high heat, then add the chopped onion, diced chiles, minced ginger, minced garlic, cassia bark, green cardamom pods, whole cloves, black peppercorns, salt, diced tomatoes, tomato paste, turmeric, chili powder, ground coriander seeds, and water. 2. Cover the slow cooker and let it cook on high for 1 to 2 hours, or on low for 3 hours, until the tomatoes have softened and broken down. 3. After cooking, carefully remove the cassia bark (this step is crucial, as grinding it into the sauce will darken the final dish) and blend the mixture using an immersion blender or a standard blender until smooth. You can strain it for a glossy finish, or leave it chunky if preferred. Return the sauce to the slow cooker.
Prepare the Chicken: 4. In a skillet, melt the ghee over medium heat. Add the cumin seeds and sauté for about 1 minute until fragrant, then pour this mixture into the sauce in the slow cooker. 5. Incorporate the diced chicken into the sauce, cover the slow cooker, and cook on high for 2 hours or on low for 4 hours until the chicken is fully cooked. 6. Once the chicken is done, mix in the honey, dried fenugreek leaves, and cream (if using). To thicken the sauce, you can switch the cooker to high and let it reduce with the lid off for a while. Just before serving, enhance the dish with a pat of butter, an additional drizzle of cream, and a sprinkle of coriander leaves (if desired).

Gran's Big Potluck

Prep time: 20 minutes | Cook time: 10 to 12 hours | Serves 10 to 15

- 2½ to 3 pounds (1.1 to 1.4 kg) stewing hen, cut into pieces
- ½ pound (227 g) stewing beef, cubed
- 1 (½-pound / 227-g) veal shoulder or roast, cubed
- 1½ quarts water
- ½ pound (227 g) small red potatoes, cubed
- ½ pound (227 g) small onions, cut in half
- 1 cup sliced carrots
- 1 cup chopped celery
- 1 green pepper, chopped
- 1 (1-pound / 454-g) package frozen lima beans
- 1 cup fresh or frozen okra
- 1 cup whole-kernel corn
- 1 (8-ounce / 227-g) can whole tomatoes with juice
- 1 (15-ounce / 425-g) can tomato purée
- 1 teaspoon salt
- ¼ to ½ teaspoon pepper
- 1 teaspoon dry mustard
- ½ teaspoon chili powder
- ¼ cup chopped fresh parsley

1. In a large slow cooker, mix together all the ingredients except for the final five seasonings. Alternatively, you can split the mixture into two medium slow cookers. 2. Secure the lid and set the cooker to low heat. Allow it to cook for 10 to 12 hours. In the final hour, stir in the seasonings to enhance the flavor.

Garlicky Lemon and Thyme Turkey

Prep time: 15 minutes | Cook time: 6 to 8 hours | Serves 6

- 8 cloves garlic, peeled
- Grated zest of 4 lemons
- 2 teaspoons fresh thyme leaves
- Salt and freshly ground black
- pepper
- ¼ cup extra-virgin olive oil
- 6 turkey legs, skin removed
- ½ cup dry white wine
- 1 cup chicken broth

1. In a food processor or blender, combine garlic, zest, thyme, 1½ teaspoons of salt, ½ teaspoon of pepper, and oil until a smooth paste forms. Apply this mixture generously to the turkey, then place the turkey into the slow cooker. 2. In the insert of a 5- to 7-quart slow cooker, add the wine and chicken broth. 3. Secure the lid and cook on low for 6 to 8 hours, or until the turkey is fully cooked and reaches an internal temperature of 175ºF (79ºC) on an instant-read thermometer. 4. Carefully take the turkey legs out of the sauce and cover them with aluminum foil. Strain the sauce through a fine-mesh sieve into a saucepan and bring it to a boil over medium heat. 5. Adjust the sauce's flavor with additional salt and pepper before serving.

Asian-Style Chicken Salad with Crunch

Prep time: 25 minutes | Cook time: 3 to 8 hours | Serves 8

Marinade:

- 3 cloves minced garlic
- 1 tablespoon fresh ginger, grated
- 1 teaspoon dried red pepper flakes
- 2 tablespoons honey
- 3 tablespoons low-sodium soy sauce
- 6 boneless, skinless chicken breast halves

Dressing:

- ½ cup rice wine vinegar
- 1 clove garlic, minced
- 1 teaspoon fresh grated ginger
- 1 tablespoon honey

Salad:

- 1 large head iceberg lettuce, shredded
- 2 carrots, julienned
- ½ cup chopped roasted
- peanuts
- ¼ cup chopped cilantro
- ½ package mei fun noodles, fried in hot oil

1. Mix marinade ingredients in a small bowl. 2. Place chicken in crock pot and pour marinade over chicken, coating each piece well. 3. Cover. Cook on low 6 to 8 hours, or on high 3 to 4 hours.

4. Remove chicken from crock pot and cool. Reserve juices. Shred chicken into bite-sized pieces. 5. In a small bowl, combine the dressing ingredients with ½ cup of the juice from the crock pot. 6. In a large serving bowl toss together the shredded chicken, lettuce, carrots, peanuts, cilantro, and noodles. 7. Just before serving, drizzle with the salad dressing. Toss well and serve.

Mediterranean Herb-Infused Turkey Breast

Prep time: 20 minutes | Cook time: 7½ hours | Serves 8

- 1 (4-pound / 1.8-kg) turkey breast, trimmed of fat
- ½ cup chicken stock
- 2 tablespoons fresh lemon juice
- 2 cups chopped onions
- ½ cup pitted Kalamata olives
- ½ cup oil-packed sun-dried tomatoes, drained and thinly sliced
- 1 clove garlic, minced
- 1 teaspoon dried oregano
- ½ teaspoon ground cinnamon
- ½ teaspoon ground dill
- ¼ teaspoon ground nutmeg
- ¼ teaspoon cayenne pepper
- 1 teaspoon sea salt
- ¼ teaspoon black pepper
- 3 tablespoons all-purpose flour

1. Place the turkey breast, ¼ cup of the chicken stock, lemon juice, onions, Kalamata olives, garlic, and sun-dried tomatoes into the crock pot. Sprinkle with the oregano, cinnamon, dill, nutmeg, cayenne pepper, salt, and black pepper. Cover and cook on low for 7 hours. 2. Combine the remaining ¼ cup chicken stock and the flour in a small bowl. Whisk until smooth. Stir into the crock pot. Cover and cook on low for an additional 30 minutes. 3. Serve hot over rice, pasta, potatoes, or another starch of your choice.

Can-You-Believe-It's-So-Simple Salsa Chicken

Prep time: 5 minutes | Cook time: 5 to 8 hours | Serves 4 to 6

- 4 to 6 boneless, skinless chicken breast halves
- 1 (16-ounce / 454-g) jar chunky-style salsa, your
- choice of heat
- 2 cups shredded cheese, your choice of flavor

1. Put the chicken into the slow cooker and pour salsa on top, ensuring the chicken is well covered. 2. Secure the lid and cook on low for 5 to 8 hours, or until the chicken is tender and juicy. 3. Serve individual portions topped with shredded cheese for added flavor.

Barbecued Chicken Legs

Prep time: 15 minutes | Cook time: 8 hours | Serves 8

- 10 chicken legs, skin removed
- 1 teaspoon salt
- ½ teaspoon freshly ground black pepper
- 2 tablespoons unsalted butter
- 1 medium onion, finely chopped
- 1 clove garlic, minced
- 1 tablespoon Dijon mustard
- 1 tablespoon Worcestershire sauce
- 1½ cups ketchup
- ½ cup chicken broth
- ½ cup firmly packed light brown sugar
- ¼ cup molasses
- ½ teaspoon hot sauce

1. Prepare the insert of a 5- to 7-quart slow cooker by spraying it with nonstick cooking spray or lining it with a slow-cooker liner following the manufacturer's instructions. 2. Season the chicken legs with salt and pepper, ensuring an even coating, then place them into the slow cooker insert. 3. In a large saucepan over medium-high heat, melt the butter. Once melted, add the onion and garlic, sautéing until the onion becomes tender, which should take about 3 minutes. 4. Incorporate the remaining ingredients into the saucepan, stirring well to combine everything. Pour this sauce mixture over the chicken in the slow cooker. Cook on low for 8 hours, or until the chicken is tender and fully cooked. After cooking, remove the lid and skim off any excess fat from the top. 5. Keep the cooker on the warm setting and serve the chicken directly from it for a delicious meal.

Honey-Dijon Turkey Tenderloins with Raisin Stuffing

Prep time: 15 minutes | Cook time: 7 hours | Serves 2

- 5 slices oatmeal bread, cubed
- 1 small onion, chopped
- 2 garlic cloves, minced
- ½ cup raisins
- 1 egg
- 2 tablespoons butter, melted
- ½ teaspoon salt
- ⅛ teaspoon freshly ground black pepper
- ½ cup chicken stock
- 2 (1 pounds / 454 g) turkey tenderloins
- 2 tablespoons Dijon mustard
- 2 tablespoons honey
- 1 teaspoon poultry seasoning

1. In the crock pot, combine the bread, onion, garlic, raisins, egg, butter, salt, and pepper, and mix. Drizzle the stock over everything and stir gently to coat. 2. On a platter, rub the turkey tenderloins with the Dijon mustard and honey, and then sprinkle with the poultry seasoning. Place the tenderloins over the bread mixture in the crock pot. 3. Cover and cook on low for 6 to 7 hours, until the turkey registers 160ºF (71ºC) on a meat thermometer. 4. Slice the turkey and serve it with the stuffing.

Braised Chicken with Niçzise Olives

Prep time: 15 minutes | Cook time: 4 to 5 hours | Serves 6

- ½ cup all-purpose flour
- Salt and freshly ground black pepper
- 8 chicken thighs, skin and bones removed
- ¼ cup extra-virgin olive oil
- 4 garlic cloves, sliced
- ¾ cup dry white wine or vermouth
- 1½ cup chicken broth
- 1 cup pitted Niçoise olives
- 1 lemon, cut into ½-inch-thick slices
- 1 bay leaf

1. In a large plastic bag, mix together the flour, ½ teaspoon of salt, and ½ teaspoon of pepper. Place the chicken in the bag and shake well to ensure it's evenly coated. In a large skillet, heat the oil over high heat. 2. Add the coated chicken to the skillet and brown it on all sides for about 7 to 10 minutes. 3. Once browned, transfer the chicken to the insert of a 5- to 7-quart slow cooker. In the same skillet, add the garlic and sauté until it becomes fragrant, which should take around 30 seconds. 4. Pour in the wine to deglaze the skillet, scraping up any flavorful browned bits stuck to the bottom. Transfer this mixture to the slow cooker along with the chicken. Add the remaining ingredients and stir well to combine. Cover the slow cooker and set it to low, cooking for 4 to 5 hours until the chicken is tender. 5. Before serving, taste and adjust the seasoning with additional salt and pepper as needed.

Zesty Garlic-Lime Chicken

Prep time: 10 minutes | Cook time: 4 to 8 hours | Serves 5

- 5 chicken breast halves
- ½ cup soy sauce
- ¼ to ⅓ cup lime juice, according to your taste preference
- 1 tablespoon Worcestershire
- sauce
- 2 garlic cloves, minced, or 1 teaspoon garlic powder
- ½ teaspoon dry mustard
- ½ teaspoon ground pepper

1. Place chicken in crock pot. 2. Combine remaining ingredients and pour over chicken. 3. Cover. Cook on high 4 to 6 hours, or on low 6 to 8 hours.

Savory Chicken & Herb Stuffing Bake

Prep time: 20 minutes | Cook time: 4½ to 5 hours | Serves 14 to 16

- 2½ cups chicken broth
- 1 cup butter, melted
- ½ cup chopped onions
- ½ cup chopped celery
- 1 (4-ounce / 113-g) can mushrooms, stems and pieces, drained
- ¼ cup dried parsley flakes
- 1½ teaspoons rubbed sage
- 1 teaspoon poultry seasoning
- 1 teaspoon salt
- ½ teaspoon pepper
- 12 cups day-old bread cubes (½-inch pieces)
- 2 eggs
- 1 (10¾-ounce / 305-g) can cream of chicken soup
- 5 to 6 cups cubed cooked chicken

1. Combine all ingredients except bread, eggs, soup, and chicken in saucepan. Simmer for 10 minutes. 2. Place bread cubes in large bowl. 3. Combine eggs and soup. Stir into broth mixture until smooth. Pour over bread and toss well. 4. Layer half of stuffing and then half of chicken into very large crock pot (or two medium-sized cookers). Repeat layers. 5. Cover. Cook on low 4½ to 5 hours.

Spicy Buffalo Chicken Cream Sauce

Prep time: 10 minutes | Cook time: 7½ hours | Serves 2

- 1 onion, chopped
- 3 garlic cloves, minced
- 1 cup sliced cremini mushrooms
- 3 celery stalks, sliced
- 1 red bell pepper, sliced
- 2 tablespoons minced celery leaves
- 5 boneless, skinless chicken thighs, cubed
- 3 tablespoons all-purpose flour
- ½ teaspoon dried marjoram
- leaves
- ½ teaspoon salt
- ⅛ teaspoon freshly ground black pepper
- 1¼ cups chicken stock
- ¼ cup Buffalo wing hot sauce
- 1 bay leaf
- 3 ounces (85 g) cream cheese, cubed
- ¼ cup sour cream
- ¼ cup crumbled blue cheese

1. In the crock pot, combine the onion, garlic, mushrooms, celery, bell pepper, and celery leaves. 2. In a large bowl, toss the chicken thighs with the flour, marjoram, salt, and pepper, and place them on top of the vegetables in the crock pot. 3. In a small bowl, mix the stock with the hot sauce and bay leaf; pour the mixture into the crock pot. 4. Cover and cook on low for 7 hours, and then remove and discard the bay leaf. 5. Stir in the cream cheese and sour cream, cover, and cook on low for 20 to 30 minutes more, or until the cream cheese is melted. Gently stir. 6. Stir in the blue cheese and serve.

Citrus-Glazed Chicken with Mandarin Oranges

Prep time: 20 minutes | Cook time: 4½ to 5½ hours | Serves 4

- 4 boneless, skinless chicken breast halves
- 1 medium onion, thinly sliced
- ¼ cup orange juice concentrate
- 1 teaspoon poultry seasoning
- ½ teaspoon salt
- 1 (11-ounce / 312-g) can mandarin oranges, drained, with 3 tablespoons juice reserved
- 2 tablespoons flour

1. Place chicken in crock pot. 2. Combine onion, orange juice concentrate, poultry seasoning, and salt. Pour over chicken. 3. Cover. Cook on low 4 to 5 hours. 4. Remove chicken and keep warm. Reserve cooking juices. 5. In a saucepan, combine 3 tablespoons reserved mandarin orange juice and flour. Stir until smooth. 6. Stir in chicken cooking juices. Bring to a boil. Stir and cook for 2 minutes to thicken. 7. Stir in mandarin oranges. Pour over chicken. 8. Serve.

Lemon Garlic Chicken Thighs

Prep time: 15 minutes | Cook time: 7 to 8 hours | Serves 4

- ¼ cup extra-virgin olive oil, divided
- 1½ pounds (680 g) boneless chicken thighs
- 1 teaspoon paprika
- Salt, for seasoning
- Freshly ground black pepper,
- for seasoning
- 1 sweet onion, chopped
- 4 garlic cloves, thinly sliced
- ½ cup chicken broth
- 2 tablespoons freshly squeezed lemon juice
- ½ cup Greek yogurt

1. Lightly grease the insert of the crock pot with 1 tablespoon of the olive oil. 2. Season the thighs with paprika, salt, and pepper. 3. In a large skillet over medium-high heat, heat the remaining olive oil. Add the chicken and brown for 5 minutes, turning once. 4. Transfer the chicken to the insert and add the onion, garlic, broth, and lemon juice. 5. Cover and cook on low for 7 to 8 hours. 6. Stir in the yogurt and serve.

Tex-Mex Chicken and Beans

Prep time: 20 minutes | Cook time: 8 hours | Serves 4

- 1 cup dried pinto beans, rinsed
- 1 (11-ounce / 312-g) jar mild or medium salsa (1½ cups)
- 2 tablespoons chopped chipotle chile in adobo sauce
- 2 tablespoons all-purpose flour
- 1 cup water
- 1½ pounds (680 g) boneless, skinless chicken thighs (about 8)
- Coarse salt and freshly ground pepper
- 1 red onion, chopped
- 1 red bell pepper, chopped
- Sour cream, finely chopped jalapeño, hot sauce, and tortilla strips or chips, for serving

1. In a large bowl, add the beans and cover them with several inches of water. Refrigerate the bowl, covered, overnight, then drain the beans. 2. Preheat your 5- to 6-quart slow cooker. 3. In the slow cooker, combine the beans, salsa, chiles, flour, and water, stirring well to mix everything together. Season the chicken with salt and pepper and place it on top of the bean mixture. Then, scatter the onion and bell pepper over the chicken. Cover the cooker and set it to low for 8 hours or high for 4 hours. 4. Once cooking is complete, remove the chicken from the slow cooker and place it on a large plate. Using two forks, shred the chicken into large pieces and return it to the stew. Serve the dish hot with sour cream, jalapeños, hot sauce, and tortilla strips on the side.

Spicy Buffalo Chicken with Garlic and Coconut Oil

Prep time: 10 minutes | Cook time: 6 hours | Serves 4

- 3 tablespoons olive oil, divided
- 1 pound (454 g) boneless chicken breasts
- 1 cup hot sauce
- ½ sweet onion, finely chopped
- ⅓ cup coconut oil, melted
- ¼ cup water
- 1 teaspoon minced garlic
- 2 tablespoons chopped fresh parsley, for garnish

1. Lightly grease the insert of the crock pot with 1 tablespoon of the olive oil. 2. In a large skillet over medium-high heat, heat the remaining 2 tablespoons of the olive oil. Add the chicken and brown for 5 minutes, turning once. 3. Transfer the chicken to the insert and arrange in one layer on the bottom. 4. In a small bowl, whisk together the hot sauce, onion, coconut oil, water, and garlic. Pour the mixture over the chicken. 5. Cover and cook on low for 6 hours. 6. Serve topped with the parsley.

Spanish Chicken

Prep time: 10 minutes | Cook time: 8 hours | Serves 2

- 2 bone-in, skinless chicken quarters
- 2 teaspoons chili powder
- ½ teaspoon ground sweet paprika
- ½ teaspoon salt
- ⅛ teaspoon ground cayenne pepper
- 1 onion, chopped
- 1 green bell pepper, chopped
- 2 garlic cloves, minced
- ⅔ cup long grain brown rice
- 1 (14 ounces / 397 g) can diced tomatoes, undrained
- 1 cup chicken stock
- 1 tablespoon freshly squeezed lemon juice
- ½ teaspoon lemon zest
- 1 pinch saffron threads
- ¼ cup sliced green olives
- 1 cup frozen green peas, thawed

1. On a platter, season the chicken by sprinkling it with chili powder, paprika, salt, and cayenne pepper, then rub the spices thoroughly into the chicken. 2. In the slow cooker, combine the onion, bell pepper, garlic, and rice, then place the seasoned chicken quarters on top. 3. In a medium bowl, whisk together the tomatoes, stock, lemon juice, lemon zest, and saffron. Allow this mixture to sit for 5 minutes before pouring it over the chicken in the slow cooker. Finally, add the olives on top. 4. Cover the slow cooker and set it to low, cooking for 7 to 8 hours, or until the chicken reaches an internal temperature of 165ºF (74ºC) when checked with a meat thermometer. 5. After cooking, stir in the peas, cover, and cook on high for an additional 10 minutes before serving.

Savory Turkey Breast with Creamy Mushroom Sauce

Prep time: 15 minutes | Cook time: 7 to 8 hours | Serves 12

- 1 large boneless, skinless turkey breast, halved
- 2 tablespoons butter, melted
- 2 tablespoons dried parsley
- ½ teaspoon dried oregano
- ½ teaspoon salt
- ¼ teaspoon black pepper
- ½ cup white wine
- 1 cup sliced fresh mushrooms
- 2 tablespoons cornstarch
- ¼ cup cold water

1. Place turkey in crock pot. Brush with butter. 2. Mix together parsley, oregano, salt, pepper, and wine. Pour over turkey. 3. Top with mushrooms. 4. Cover. Cook on low 7 to 8 hours. 5. Remove turkey and keep warm. 6. Skim any fat from cooking juices. 7. In a saucepan, combine cornstarch and water until smooth. Gradually add cooking juices. Bring to a boil. Cook and stir 2 minutes until thickened. 8. Slice turkey and serve with sauce.

Turkey Braised in Tomato Sauce

Prep time: 20 minutes | Cook time: 3 hours | Serves 8

- 6 strips thick-cut bacon, cut into ½-inch pieces
- 1 medium onion, finely chopped
- 1 teaspoon dried basil
- 1 pound (454 g) cremini mushrooms, quartered
- 1½ teaspoons salt
- ½ teaspoon freshly ground black pepper
- 1 (28- to 32-ounce / 794- to 907-g) can crushed tomatoes
- ½ cup finely chopped fresh Italian parsley
- 4 turkey thighs, skin removed

1. In a skillet over medium heat, cook the bacon until it starts to crisp and releases some fat. Then, add the onion and basil, sautéing until the onion becomes tender, which should take about 3 minutes. 2. Incorporate the mushrooms, salt, and pepper, and continue to sauté until the mushrooms develop some color, around 7 to 10 minutes. Transfer this mixture to the insert of a 5- to 7-quart slow cooker. Stir in the tomatoes and parsley, mixing well, then place the thighs in the sauce. 3. Cover the slow cooker and set it to high heat, cooking for 3 hours, or until the thighs are fully cooked and reach an internal temperature of 175ºF (79ºC) when checked with an instant-read thermometer. Skim any excess fat from the surface of the sauce. Remove the thighs, discarding the bones. 4. Cut the meat into portions suitable for serving and return it to the sauce. 5. Keep the cooker on the warm setting and serve directly from there.

Cuban-Style Chicken and Black Beans with Mango

Prep time: 20 minutes | Cook time: 7 hours | Serves 2

- 2 boneless, skinless chicken breasts
- 2 teaspoons jerk seasoning
- ½ teaspoon salt
- 1 onion, chopped
- 2 garlic cloves, minced
- 1 serrano pepper, minced
- 1 (14 ounces / 397 g) can black beans, rinsed and drained
- ⅔ cup long grain brown rice
- 1⅓ cups chicken stock
- 2 tablespoons freshly squeezed lime juice
- 1 tablespoon honey
- 1 bay leaf
- 2 tablespoons minced black olives
- 1 mango, peeled and cubed

1. On a platter, sprinkle the chicken breasts with the jerk seasoning and salt; set aside. 2. In the crock pot, combine the onion, garlic, serrano pepper, black beans, and rice. 3. Pour the stock, lime juice, and honey into the crock pot, and mix. Add the bay leaf. 4. Top with the chicken and sprinkle with the olives. 5. Cover and cook on low for 6 to 7 hours, or until the chicken registers 160ºF (71ºC) on a meat thermometer. 6. Remove the chicken from the crock pot to a clean platter. Remove the bay leaf from the crock pot and discard. 7. Stir the mango into the mixture in the crock pot, and serve with the chicken.

Delicious Chicken

Prep time: 10 minutes | Cook time: 8 to 10 hours | Serves 6

- 3 whole chicken breasts, skin removed and halved
- 1 (10¾-ounce / 305-g) can low-sodium condensed cream of chicken soup
- ½ cup cooking sherry
- 1 (4-ounce / 113-g) can
- sliced mushrooms, drained
- 1 teaspoon Worcestershire sauce
- 1 teaspoon dried tarragon leaves or dried rosemary
- ¼ teaspoon garlic powder

1. Rinse the chicken breasts under cold water and thoroughly pat them dry. Place the chicken breasts into the slow cooker. 2. In a separate bowl, mix together the remaining ingredients and pour this sauce over the chicken, ensuring that each piece is well coated. 3. Cover the slow cooker and set it to cook on low for 8 to 10 hours, or on high for 4 to 5 hours. 4. Once cooked, serve the chicken hot.

Bacon-Mushroom Chicken

Prep time: 15 minutes | Cook time: 7 to 8 hours | Serves 8

- 3 tablespoons coconut oil, divided
- ¼ pound (113 g) bacon, diced
- 2 pounds (907 g) chicken (breasts, thighs, drumsticks)
- 2 cups quartered button
- mushrooms
- 1 sweet onion, diced
- 1 tablespoon minced garlic
- ½ cup chicken broth
- 2 teaspoons chopped thyme
- 1 cup coconut cream

1. Grease the insert of the slow cooker lightly with 1 tablespoon of coconut oil. 2. In a large skillet set over medium-high heat, melt the remaining 2 tablespoons of coconut oil. 3. Add the bacon to the skillet and cook until it becomes crispy, which should take about 5 minutes. Use a slotted spoon to remove the bacon and transfer it to a plate to cool. 4. In the same skillet, add the chicken and brown it for about 5 minutes, turning it once during cooking. 5. Once browned, move the chicken and bacon to the slow cooker insert, then add the mushrooms, onion, garlic, broth, and thyme to the mix. 6. Cover the slow cooker and set it to low, allowing it to cook for 7 to 8 hours. 7. After cooking, stir in the coconut cream and serve the dish hot.

Creamy Chicken and Shrimp Rice Casserole

Prep time: 20 minutes | Cook time: 3 to 8 hours | Serves 4 to 6

- 1¼ cups rice, uncooked
- ½ cup (1 stick) butter, melted
- 3 cups chicken broth
- 3 to 4 cups cut-up cooked chicken breast
- 2 (4-ounce / 113-g) cans sliced mushrooms, drained
- ⅓ cup soy sauce
- 1 (12-ounce / 340-g) package shelled frozen shrimp
- 8 green onions, chopped, 2 tablespoons reserved
- ⅔ cup slivered almonds

1. Combine rice and butter in crock pot. Stir to coat rice well. 2. Add remaining ingredients except almonds and 2 tablespoons green onions. 3. Cover. Cook on low 6 to 8 hours, or on high 3 to 4 hours, until rice is tender. 4. Sprinkle almonds and green onions over top before serving.

Quick-Fried Spicy Chicken

Prep time: 15 minutes | Cook time: 4 to 6 hours | Serves 6

Chicken:
- 2 tablespoons rapeseed oil
- 4 fresh green chiles, chopped
- 4 garlic cloves, sliced
- 4 tomatoes, chopped
- 1 teaspoon salt

Quick-Fry:
- 1 tablespoon rapeseed oil
- 1 teaspoon cumin seeds
- 1 red onion, sliced
- 1 red bell pepper, seeded and cut into chunks
- 1 green bell pepper, seeded

- ½ teaspoon turmeric
- 8 boneless chicken thighs, skinned, trimmed, and cut into chunks
- ¼ cup water

- and cut into chunks
- 2 fresh green chiles, sliced lengthwise
- 1 tomato, chopped
- ½ teaspoon salt
- 1 teaspoon garam masala

Make the Chicken:
1. Set the slow cooker to high and pour in the oil. 2. Add the chiles, garlic, chopped tomatoes, salt, and turmeric to the pot, cooking for a few minutes until fragrant. Then, add the chicken pieces along with the water, stirring to ensure the chicken is well coated. 3. Cover the slow cooker and cook on high for 4 hours, or switch to low for 6 hours.

Make the Quick-Fry:
4. When you're ready to serve, heat oil in a sauté pan and add the cumin seeds, cooking until they become fragrant, about 1 minute. 5. Next, toss in the onion, red and green pepper chunks, chiles,

tomato, salt, and garam masala, sautéing for about 5 minutes. 6. Pour this pepper mixture into the crock pot with the chicken, cover, and continue to cook on high for an additional 15 minutes with the lid off, allowing the peppers to soften to your liking and the sauce to reduce and thicken.

Turkey in the crock pot

Prep time: 5 minutes | Cook time: 1 to 5 hours | Serves 6 to 8

- 1 (3- to 5-pound / 1.4- to 2.3-kg) bone-in turkey breast
- Salt and pepper to taste
- 2 carrots, cut in chunks
- 1 onion, cut in eighths
- 2 ribs celery, cut in chunks

1. Rinse the turkey breast under cold water and pat it dry thoroughly. Generously season the inside with salt. 2. Arrange the vegetables at the bottom of the slow cooker and sprinkle them with pepper. Place the seasoned turkey breast on top of the vegetables. 3. Cover the slow cooker and cook on high for 1 to 3 hours, or on low for 4 to 5 hours, until the turkey is tender but remains moist and not overly soft.

Herb-Infused Chicken Thighs in White Wine Sauce

Prep time: 20 minutes | Cook time: 7 hours | Serves 2

- 7 bone-in, skin-on chicken thighs
- 2 tablespoons Dijon mustard
- 1 teaspoon ground paprika
- 1 teaspoon dried thyme leaves
- ½ teaspoon dried basil leaves
- 3 tablespoons all-purpose
- flour
- ½ teaspoon salt
- ⅛ teaspoon freshly ground black pepper
- 1 tablespoon extra-virgin olive oil
- ½ cup dry white wine
- ¼ cup chicken stock

1. On a platter, loosen the skin from the chicken. 2. In a small bowl, mix the mustard, paprika, thyme, and basil, and rub the mixture onto the chicken meat, beneath the skin. Spread the chicken skin back over this mixture and secure with toothpicks. 3. Sprinkle the chicken with the flour, salt, and pepper. 4. In a medium skillet over medium heat, heat the oil. Add the chicken, skin-side down, and brown, about 4 minutes. Do not turn the chicken over. Remove the chicken from the skillet to the crock pot. 5. Add the wine and stock to the skillet and bring to a simmer, stirring to remove the pan drippings. 6. Pour the wine mixture over the chicken in the crock pot. 7. Cover and cook on low for 7 hours, or until the chicken registers 165ºF (74ºC) on a meat thermometer. 8. Remove the toothpicks and serve.

Chicken Dijonaise

Prep time: 20 minutes | Cook time: 4 to 5 hours | Serves 8

- 3 to 4 pounds (1.4 to 1.8 kg) chicken parts (breasts, thighs, legs, or any combination), skin removed
- Salt and freshly ground black pepper
- 3 tablespoons extra-virgin olive oil
- 4 cloves garlic, minced
- 8 ounces (227 g) cipollini onions
- 1 pound (454 g) button mushrooms, cut in half if large
- 1 (16-ounce / 454-g) package frozen artichoke hearts, defrosted and quartered
- ½ cup dry white wine or vermouth
- 1½ cups chicken broth
- ⅔ cup Dijon mustard
- 1 bay leaf

1. Evenly season the chicken with 1½ teaspoons of salt and ½ teaspoon of pepper. In a large skillet, heat the oil over high heat. Add the chicken in batches, browning it on all sides. 2. Once browned, transfer the chicken to the insert of a 5- to 7-quart slow cooker. In the same skillet, add the garlic and onions, sautéing until the onions start to brown, which should take about 4 minutes. Then, add the mushrooms and continue to sauté until the moisture in the pan begins to evaporate, approximately 3 to 4 minutes. 3. Incorporate the artichoke hearts into the skillet and sauté for an additional 3 to 4 minutes to give them some color. 4. Pour in the wine to deglaze the pan, scraping up any browned bits stuck to the bottom. Transfer all the contents of the skillet into the slow cooker. In a small bowl, combine the broth and mustard, whisking until well blended. 5. Pour the broth mixture into the slow cooker and add the bay leaf, stirring everything together. Cover the cooker and set it to low, cooking for 4 to 5 hours, or until the chicken is tender. 6. Before serving, taste and adjust the seasoning with additional salt and pepper as desired.

Tangy Carolina Vinegar BBQ Chicken

Prep time: 10 minutes | Cook time: 4 hours | Serves 6

- 2 cups water
- 1 cup white vinegar
- ¼ cup sugar
- 1 tablespoon reduced-sodium chicken base
- 1 teaspoon crushed red
- pepper flakes
- ¾ teaspoon salt
- 1½ pounds (680 g) boneless skinless chicken breasts
- 6 whole wheat hamburger buns, split (optional)

1. In a small bowl, mix the first six ingredients. Place chicken in a 3-quart crock pot; add vinegar mixture. Cook, covered, on low 4 to 5 hours or until chicken is tender. 2. Remove chicken; cool slightly. Reserve 1 cup cooking juices; discard remaining juices. Shred chicken with two forks. Return meat and reserved cooking juices to crock pot; heat through. If desired, serve chicken mixture on buns.

Layered Chicken and Black Bean Torta

Prep time: 20 minutes | Cook time: 4 to 5 hours | Serves 6

- 1 pound (454 g) uncooked boneless, skinless chicken breasts
- 1 medium onion
- ½ teaspoon garlic salt
- ¼ teaspoon black pepper
- 1 (15-ounce / 425-g) can ranch-style black beans
- 1 (15-ounce / 425-g) can low-sodium diced tomatoes
- with green chilies
- 4 tortillas
- 1½ cups shredded low-fat Cheddar cheese
- Salsa
- Fat-free sour cream
- Lettuce
- Tomatoes
- Nonfat cooking spray

1. Cut chicken in small pieces. Brown with onion in nonstick skillet. Drain well. 2. Season with garlic salt and pepper. Stir in beans and tomatoes. 3. Place strips of foil on bottom and up sides of crock pot, forming an X. Spray foil and cooker lightly with nonfat cooking spray. 4. Place 1 tortilla on bottom of cooker. Spoon on one-third of chicken mixture and one-quarter of the cheese. 5. Repeat layers, ending with a tortilla sprinkled with cheese on top. 6. Cover. Cook on low 4 to 5 hours. 7. Remove to platter using foil strips as handles. Gently pull out foil and discard. 8. Serve with salsa, sour cream, lettuce, and tomatoes.

Sweet and Spicy Asian Stewed Chicken

Prep time: 20 minutes | Cook time: 4 hours | Serves 4 to 6

- 1 whole chicken, cut up
- 3 tablespoons hot sweet mustard, or 2 tablespoons hot mustard and 1 tablespoon
- honey
- 2 tablespoons soy sauce
- 1 teaspoon ground ginger
- 1 teaspoon cumin

1. Wash chicken and place in crock pot. Pat dry. 2. Mix the remaining ingredients in a bowl. Taste and adjust seasonings if you want. Pour over chicken. 3. Cover and cook on high for at least 4 hours, or until tender.

Sweet Citrus Roasted Chicken

Prep time: 5 minutes | Cook time: 8 hours | Serves 4 to 6

- 1 lemon
- 1 whole roasting chicken, rinsed
- ½ cup orange juice
- ½ cup honey

1. Pierce lemon with fork. Place in chicken cavity. Place chicken in crock pot. 2. Combine orange juice and honey. Pour over chicken. 3. Cover. Cook on low 8 hours. Remove lemon and squeeze over chicken. 4. Carve chicken and serve.

Stuffed Chicken Parmigiana

Prep time: 30 minutes | Cook time: 2½ to 3 hours | Serves 6

- 2 tablespoons extra-virgin olive oil
- 1 large onion, finely chopped
- Pinch of red pepper flakes
- 1½ teaspoons dried oregano
- ½ teaspoon dried basil
- ½ cup dry red wine
- 1 (28-ounce / 794-g) can crushed tomatoes, with their juice
- 6 chicken breast halves, skinned and boned
- 1½ teaspoons salt
- ½ teaspoon freshly ground black pepper
- 1 large egg
- 1 cup fresh bread crumbs
- ½ cup finely shredded Parmigiano-Reggiano cheese, plus additional, for garnish
- ½ cup finely shredded Fontina cheese
- ½ cup finely shredded Mozzarella cheese
- ½ cup finely chopped fresh Italian parsley

1. In a large skillet, heat the oil over medium-high heat. Add the onion, red pepper flakes, oregano, and basil, sautéing until the onion is tender, about 3 minutes. Pour in the wine and allow it to boil until it reduces to approximately 2 tablespoons. Transfer this mixture to the insert of a 5- to 7-quart slow cooker and add the tomatoes, stirring to combine. 2. Place the chicken breasts shiny-side up between two sheets of plastic wrap and gently pound them to an even thickness. Season the chicken with salt and pepper on both sides. In a small bowl, mix together the egg, bread crumbs, cheeses, and parsley until well combined. 3. Spread the filling mixture over the chicken breasts, then roll them up tightly. Carefully place the rolled chicken into the tomato sauce in the slow cooker. Cover and cook on low for 2½ to 3 hours, or until the chicken is fully cooked,

reaching an internal temperature of 170ºF (77ºC) when measured with an instant-read thermometer. Once cooked, gently transfer the chicken to a serving platter and cover with aluminum foil to keep warm. 4. Using a serrated knife, slice the chicken and serve each piece in a pool of the sauce. Garnish with additional Parmigiano-Reggiano cheese for extra flavor.

Hearty Chicken and Italian Sausage Cacciatore

Prep time: 35 minutes | Cook time: 8 hours | Serves 4 to 6

- 1 large green pepper, sliced in 1-inch strips
- 1 cup sliced mushrooms
- 1 medium onion, sliced in rings
- 1 pound (454 g) skinless, boneless chicken breasts,
- browned
- 1 pound (454 g) Italian sausage, browned
- ½ teaspoon dried oregano
- ½ teaspoon dried basil
- 1½ cups Italian-style tomato sauce

1. Layer vegetables in crock pot. 2. Top with meat. 3. Sprinkle with oregano and basil. 4. Top with tomato sauce. 5. Cover. Cook on low 8 hours. 6. Remove cover during last 30 minutes of cooking time to allow sauce to cook off and thicken. 7. Serve.

Crock Pot Stuffing with Poultry

Prep time: 15 minutes | Cook time: 7 to 9 hours | Serves 18

- 1 large loaf dried low-fat bread, cubed
- 2 cups chopped, cooked turkey or chicken, skin removed
- 1 large onion, chopped
- 3 ribs celery with leaves, chopped
- ¼ cup butter, melted
- 4 cups fat-free chicken broth
- 1 tablespoon poultry seasoning
- 1 teaspoon salt
- 4 eggs, beaten
- ½ teaspoon black pepper

1. Combine all the ingredients in a bowl, mixing them thoroughly. Pour the mixture into the slow cooker. 2. Cover the slow cooker and cook on high for 1 hour. After that, reduce the heat to low and continue cooking for 6 to 8 hours.

Chicken Divan

Prep time: 15 minutes | Cook time: 3 to 4 hours | Serves 4

- 4 boneless, skinless chicken breast halves
- 4 cups chopped broccoli, fresh or frozen
- 2 (10¾-ounce / 305-g) cans cream of chicken soup
- 1 cup mayonnaise
- ½ to 1 teaspoon curry powder, depending upon your taste preference

1. Arrange the chicken breasts in the bottom of the slow cooker. 2. Layer the broccoli evenly on top of the chicken. 3. In a small mixing bowl, combine the soup, mayonnaise, and curry powder, stirring until well blended. Pour this mixture over the chicken and broccoli, ensuring an even coating. 4. Cover the slow cooker and set it to high, cooking for 3 to 4 hours, or until the chicken and broccoli are tender but not overcooked. Serve the dish hot.

Chicken Azteca

Prep time: 20 minutes | Cook time: 2½ to 6½ hours | Serves 10 to 12

- 2 (15-ounce / 425-g) cans black beans, drained
- 4 cups frozen corn kernels
- 2 garlic cloves, minced
- ¾ teaspoon ground cumin
- 2 cups chunky salsa, divided
- 10 skinless, boneless chicken breast halves
- 2 (8-ounce / 227-g) packages cream cheese, cubed
- Rice, cooked
- Shredded Cheddar cheese

1. In the slow cooker, mix together the beans, corn, garlic, cumin, and half of the salsa until well combined. 2. Place the chicken breasts on top of the mixture and pour the remaining salsa over them. 3. Cover the slow cooker and cook on high for 2 to 3 hours, or on low for 4 to 6 hours. 4. Once cooked, remove the chicken and cut it into bite-sized pieces, then return it to the cooker. 5. Stir in the cream cheese and continue to cook on high until the cream cheese is fully melted and incorporated. 6. Serve the chicken and sauce over cooked rice, and sprinkle with shredded cheese on top.

Chapter **4**

Beef, Pork, and Lamb

Chapter 4 Beef, Pork, and Lamb

Tropical Pineapple Pork Ribs

Prep time: 10 minutes | Cook time: 6 to 8 hours | Serves 4

- 8 country-style pork ribs
- Black pepper to taste
- ¼ teaspoon paprika
- 1 (20-ounce / 567-g)

- unsweetened pineapple tidbits
- 2 tablespoons Dijon mustard
- 2 tablespoons fast-cooking tapioca (optional)

1. Slice ribs into 8 sections. Place in crock pot sprayed with nonfat cooking spray. 2. Combine remaining ingredients. Pour over ribs. 3. Cover. Cook on low 6 to 8 hours. 4. If you wish, 30 minutes before the end of the cooking time, stir in tapioca in order to thicken the cooking juices.

Bacon-Wrapped Smothered Pork Chops

Prep time: 20 minutes | Cook time: 7 to 8 hours | Serves 6 to 8

- 6 strips bacon, cut into ½-inch pieces
- ¼ cup all-purpose flour
- 1 teaspoon salt
- ½ teaspoon freshly ground black pepper
- 8 center-cut ¾-inch-thick pork chops
- 4 tablespoons (½ stick) unsalted butter

- 4 large onions, cut into ¼-inch-thick slices
- 1 teaspoon dried sage leaves, crushed in the palm of your hand
- ½ teaspoon dried thyme
- 2 tablespoons sugar
- 1 cup beef broth
- 2 cups chicken broth

1. Cook the bacon in a large skillet until crisp and remove it to paper towels to drain. Combine the flour, salt, and pepper in a zipper-top plastic bag, add the chops, and shake to coat. 2. Add the chops to the bacon drippings and brown on both sides. Transfer the chops to the insert of a 5- to 7-quart crock pot. If the chops don't fit snugly in one layer, put some on top of each other. 3. Melt the butter in the same skillet over medium-high heat. Add the onions, sage, thyme, and sugar and sauté until the onions begin to turn golden but not brown. Pour the beef broth into the skillet and scrape up any browned bits from the bottom of the pan. Transfer the contents of the skillet to the slow-cooker insert and add the chicken broth. 4. Cover the crock pot and cook on low for 7 to 8 hours, until the pork is tender. Stir in the bacon. 5. Serve the pork chops covered with some of the sauce.

Spiced Slow-Cooked North Indian Lamb Curry

Prep time: 15 minutes | Cook time: 5 to 7 hours | Serves 6 to 8

- 3⅓ pounds (1½ kg) leg of lamb, on the bone, cut into bite-size pieces
- 7 garlic cloves, roughly chopped
- 2¾-inch piece fresh ginger, chopped
- 1 fresh green chile, roughly chopped, plus 2 fresh chiles, sliced lengthwise
- 1½ teaspoons Kashmiri chili powder
- 2 tablespoons rapeseed oil
- 4 onions, thinly sliced
- 5 tomatoes, finely diced
- 1 teaspoon sea salt

- 2 to 3 tablespoons Greek yogurt
- 1 teaspoon gram flour
- 2 teaspoons coriander seeds, ground
- 1 teaspoon cumin seeds, ground
- 1 teaspoon turmeric
- ½ teaspoon freshly ground black pepper
- Handful mint leaves, chopped
- Handful fresh coriander leaves, chopped
- ½ teaspoon garam masala

1. Put the lamb into a large mixing bowl. Crush the garlic, ginger, and green chile in a mortar and pestle. Sprinkle in the chili powder and smear over the lamb. Set aside to marinate for as long as you can leave it. (Overnight in the refrigerator is fine.) 2. When you are ready to cook, heat the crock pot to high or sauté. Add the oil and the onions, then the marinated meat, and brown it for about 5 minutes, stirring occasionally. 3. Add the chopped tomatoes and cook so they begin to break down (2 to 3 minutes). Season with salt. 4. Cover and cook on high for 4 hours, or on low for 6 hours. 5. Mix the yogurt with the gram flour, coriander seeds, cumin seeds, turmeric, black pepper, mint, and coriander leaves (keep a few mint and coriander leaves for garnish). Add this mixture to the crock pot one spoonful at a time, and stir to incorporate it fully. Cook another hour with the lid off. 6. Once cooked, add the garam masala, top with the 2 sliced chiles and the reserved mint and coriander leaves, and serve.

Gone-All-Day Dinner

Prep time: 15 minutes | Cook time: 6 to 8 hours | Serves 8

- 1 cup uncooked wild rice, rinsed and drained
- 1 cup chopped celery
- 1 cup chopped carrots
- 2 (4-ounce / 113-g) cans mushrooms, drained
- 1 large onion, chopped
- ½ cup slivered almonds
- 3 beef bouillon cubes
- 2½ teaspoons seasoned salt
- 2 pounds (907 g) boneless round steak, cut in bite-sized pieces
- 3 cups water

1. Arrange the ingredients in the slow cooker in the order specified, taking care not to stir them together. 2. Cover the slow cooker and set it to low, cooking for 6 to 8 hours. 3. Before serving, give the mixture a gentle stir to combine the flavors.

Minted Indian Meatballs

Prep time: 20 minutes | Cook time: 2 to 4 hours | Serves 6 to 8

- 1¾ pounds (794 g) lean ground lamb
- 2 teaspoons ground cumin
- 2 teaspoons chili powder, divided
- 3 teaspoons garam masala
- Handful fresh mint, chopped
- ½ teaspoon ground cinnamon
- 2 teaspoons salt, divided
- 2 large onions
- 6 garlic cloves
- 2-inch piece fresh ginger
- 2 to 3 fresh green chiles
- 1 (14-ounce / 397-g) can plum tomatoes
- 1 tablespoon rapeseed oil
- 1 teaspoon turmeric
- 1 teaspoon dried fenugreek leaves
- 1 to 1¼ cups hot water
- Handful fresh coriander leaves, finely chopped

1. In a large mixing bowl, combine the lamb with cumin, 1 teaspoon of chili powder, garam masala, mint, cinnamon, and 1 teaspoon of salt. Use your hands to mix the ingredients thoroughly, ensuring the spices are evenly incorporated. 2. Lightly oil your hands to prevent the meat from sticking, then take small portions of the mixture and roll them into smooth meatballs, known as kofta. You should yield about 24 kofta; set them aside. 3. In a blender, roughly chop the onions, garlic, ginger, and chiles without puréeing them, and set the mixture aside. Then blend the tomatoes until they reach a purée consistency. 4. Set the slow cooker to high and add a bit of oil. Carefully fry the kofta in batches until they are browned all over. Once browned, transfer them to a plate lined with paper towels to drain excess oil. 5. In the same cooker, add the chopped onion mixture and sauté for 5 to 6 minutes in the remaining oil. Next, stir in the tomato purée, turmeric, dried fenugreek leaves, the

remaining 1 teaspoon of chili powder, and 1 teaspoon of salt. Mix well, then add the kofta back into the cooker, tossing gently to coat them in the sauce for a few minutes. 6. If you prefer a gravy-like consistency, add enough hot water to cover the kofta halfway; for a thicker sauce, use less water. 7. Cover the slow cooker and cook on low for 4 hours or on high for 2 to 3 hours. It's fine to let it cook longer if desired. 8. Just before serving, stir in the garam masala and chopped coriander leaves for added flavor.

Savory Pancetta and Brie Stuffed Pork Tenderloin

Prep time: 20 minutes | Cook time: 8 hours | Serves 4

- 1 tablespoon extra-virgin olive oil
- 2 (½ pounds / 227 g) pork tenderloins
- 4 ounces (113 g) pancetta, cooked crispy and chopped
- 4 ounces (113 g) triple-cream
- brie
- 1 teaspoon minced garlic
- 1 teaspoon chopped fresh basil
- ⅛ teaspoon freshly ground black pepper

1. Lightly grease the insert of the crock pot with the olive oil. 2. Place the pork on a cutting board and make a lengthwise cut, holding the knife parallel to the board, through the center of the meat without cutting right through. Open the meat up like a book and cover it with plastic wrap. 3. Pound the meat with a mallet or rolling pin until each piece is about ½ inch thick. Lay the butterflied pork on a clean work surface. 4. In a small bowl, stir together the pancetta, Brie, garlic, basil, and pepper. 5. Divide the cheese mixture between the tenderloins and spread it evenly over the meat leaving about 1 inch around the edges. 6. Roll the tenderloin up and secure with toothpicks. 7. Place the pork in the insert, cover, and cook on low for 8 hours. 8. Remove the toothpicks and serve.

Flavorful Pork Roast

Prep time: 5 minutes | Cook time: 7 hours | Serves 8 to 10

- 1 (4- to 5-pound / 1.8- to 2.3-kg) pork loin roast
- 1 large onion, sliced
- 1 bay leaf
- 2 tablespoons soy sauce
- 1 tablespoon garlic powder

1. In the slow cooker, place the roast along with the onion. Add the bay leaf, soy sauce, and garlic powder on top. 2. Cover the cooker and set it to high for 1 hour, then reduce the heat to low and cook for an additional 6 hours. 3. Once finished, slice the roast and serve.

Chili Cheese Hot Dog Delight

Prep time: 10 minutes | Cook time: 2 to 3 hours | Serves 4 to 5

- 1 package hot dogs, cut into ¾-inch slices
- 1 (28-ounce / 794-g) can baked beans
- 1 teaspoon prepared mustard
- 1 teaspoon instant minced onion
- ⅓ cup chili sauce

1. In crock pot, combine all ingredients. 2. Cover and cook on low 2 to 3 hours. 3. Serve.

Red Wine–Marinated Sirloin
Prep time: 20 minutes | Cook time: 3¼ hours | Serves 8

- 4 cups Burgundy wine
- 3 cloves garlic, minced
- 1 teaspoon dried thyme
- 1 bay leaf
- 2 tablespoons honey
- 1 teaspoon salt
- ½ teaspoon freshly ground black pepper
- 3 to 4 pounds (1.4 to 1.8 kg) beef sirloin, fat trimmed, cut into 1-inch pieces
- 6 strips thick-cut bacon, cut
- into ½-inch pieces
- 1 (15-ounce / 425-g) can double-strength beef broth
- 4 tablespoons (½ stick) unsalted butter, at room temperature
- 1 pound (454 g) small white button mushrooms
- ½ pound (227 g) pearl onions, blanched and peeled
- 3 tablespoons all-purpose flour

1. In a large zipper-top plastic bag, combine the wine, garlic, thyme, bay leaf, honey, salt, and pepper. Add the beef to the bag, seal it, and turn to coat the meat thoroughly with the marinade. Refrigerate for at least 8 hours, or up to 24 hours, turning the bag a few times during this time. 2. Once marinated, remove the meat from the bag and discard the bay leaf, setting the marinade aside. In a large skillet, cook the bacon until crispy, then transfer it to a plate lined with paper towels to drain. In the same skillet, add the beef and brown it on all sides. Once browned, transfer the meat to the insert of a 5- to 7-quart slow cooker. Pour the reserved marinade into the skillet, bringing it to a boil while scraping up any browned bits from the bottom of the pan. 3. Pour this mixture over the beef in the slow cooker and add the broth. Cover and cook on high for 3 hours, or until the meat is tender. In a separate skillet, melt 2 tablespoons of butter over medium-high heat. Add the mushrooms and onions, sautéing them until they turn golden and the liquid has evaporated. Set aside until you're ready to serve. (The mushroom and onion mixture can be refrigerated for up to 2 days.) In the same skillet, stir the remaining 2 tablespoons of butter into the flour to create a paste. 4. After the stew has finished cooking, skim any fat off the surface of the sauce, then stir in the butter and flour mixture. Add the sautéed mushrooms and onions along with the reserved bacon, mixing everything together. Cover the slow cooker and cook for an additional 15 to 20 minutes, until the sauce has thickened, before serving.

Savory Bacon-Wrapped Steak Rolls in Sauce

Prep time: 30 minutes | Cook time: 6 to 8 hours | Serves 4

- 1 (1- to 2-pound / 454 to 907-g) round steak
- 1 pound (454 g) bacon
- 1 cup ketchup
- ¼ cup brown sugar
- 1 small onion
- ¼ to ½ cup water

1. Cut round steak into long strips. Roll up each meat strip, and then wrap with a slice of bacon. Secure with a toothpick to hold the roll shape. 2. Warm remaining ingredients in saucepan, bringing to a simmer to make a sauce. 3. Place meat rolls in crock pot. Pour sauce over top. 4. Cover and cook on low 6 to 8 hours, or until the meat is tender but not overcooked.

Pork Loin Braised in Cider with Apples and Cream

Prep time: 20 minutes | Cook time: 4 hours | Serves 6 to 8

- 2 tablespoons olive oil
- ½ cup Dijon mustard
- ½ cup firmly packed light brown sugar
- 1 (2½- to 3-pound / 1.1- to 1.4-kg) pork loin roast, rolled and tied
- 1 large onion, finely sliced
- 2 teaspoons dried thyme
- ½ cup apple cider
- 1 cup beef stock
- 4 large Gala or Braeburn apples, peeled, cored, and cut into 8 wedges each
- ¾ cup heavy cream
- Salt and freshly ground black pepper
- 1 pound (454 g) buttered cooked wide egg noodles

1. In a large sauté pan over medium-high heat, warm the oil. Combine the mustard and sugar to form a paste, then spread this mixture evenly over the roast on all sides. Place the roast in the pan and brown it thoroughly on all sides. Add the onion and thyme to the sauté pan, cooking until the onion is softened, about 3 to 5 minutes. 2. Transfer the browned roast, onion, and any flavorful bits from the bottom of the pan into the insert of a 5- to 7-quart slow cooker. Pour in the cider and beef stock, then cover the crock pot and set it to cook on high for 3 hours. After 3 hours, remove the cover and add the apples and cream. Cover again and continue cooking on high for an additional hour. 3. Once cooked, take the pork out of the slow cooker and cover it with aluminum foil, allowing it to rest for 15 minutes. Season the sauce with salt and pepper to taste. Remove any strings from the roast, slice it thinly, and serve the pork over buttered noodles, drizzling both the noodles and the pork with some of the sauce.

Cuban-Style Pork Street Tacos

Prep time: 20 minutes | Cook time: 8 hours | Serves 2

- 1 teaspoon extra-virgin olive oil
- 16 ounces (454 g) pork tenderloin
- Zest of 1 orange
- Juice of 1 orange
- Zest of 1 lime
- Juice of 1 lime
- 2 garlic cloves, minced
- 1 teaspoon ground cumin
- 1 teaspoon ground coriander
- ⅛ teaspoon sea salt
- Freshly ground black pepper
- 1 red onion, halved and sliced thin
- 1 red bell pepper, cored and sliced thin
- 1 green bell pepper, cored and sliced thin
- 4 corn tortillas
- ¼ cup fresh cilantro, for garnish

1. Begin by greasing the inside of the crock pot with olive oil. 2. Place the pork tenderloin inside the crock pot. 3. In a small measuring cup, whisk together the orange zest, orange juice, lime zest, lime juice, garlic, cumin, coriander, salt, and a few grinds of black pepper. Pour this flavorful mixture over the pork. 4. Add the onion, red bell pepper, and green bell pepper to the crock pot, arranging them around and on top of the pork. 5. Cover the crock pot and set it to cook on low for 8 hours. 6. After cooking, carefully remove the pork from the crock pot and let it rest for 10 minutes. Then, shred the meat using a fork. Return the shredded pork to the crock pot and mix it with the vegetables and juices. 7. Serve the pork in warm corn tortillas, garnishing with fresh cilantro for added flavor.

Hearty Slow-Cooked Chili

Prep time: 25 minutes | Cook time: 6 to 12 hours | Serves 8 to 10

- 3 pounds (1.4 kg) beef stewing meat, browned
- 2 cloves garlic, minced
- ¼ teaspoon pepper
- ½ teaspoon cumin
- ¼ teaspoon dry mustard
- 1 (7½-ounce / 213-g) can jalapeño relish
- 1 cup beef broth
- 1 to 1½ onions, chopped, according to your taste preference
- ½ teaspoon salt
- ½ teaspoon dried oregano
- 1 tablespoon chili powder
- 1 (7-ounce / 198-g) can green chilies, chopped
- 1 (14½-ounce / 411-g) can stewed tomatoes, chopped
- 1 (15-ounce / 425-g) can tomato sauce
- 2 (15-ounce / 425-g) cans red kidney beans, rinsed and drained
- 2 (15-ounce / 425-g) cans pinto beans, rinsed and drained

1. Combine all ingredients except kidney and pinto beans in crock pot. 2. Cover. Cook on low 10 to 12 hours, or on high 6 to 7 hours. Add beans halfway through cooking time. 3. Serve.

Hearty Crock Pot Meat Loaf with Mushroom Sauce

Prep time: 20 minutes | Cook time: 7 hours | Serves 6 to 8

Meat Loaf:
- 2 pounds (907 g) ground beef or turkey
- 1 cup dry rolled oats
- Tomato juice (just enough to moisten meat if needed)
- 2 eggs
- 1 onion, diced

Sauce:
- 1 (26-ounce / 737-g) can or 2 (10¾-ounce / 305-g) cans mushroom soup
- 6 to 10 fresh mushrooms, diced

- 1 tablespoon prepared mustard
- 1 teaspoon garlic salt
- 2 tablespoons ketchup
- 1 tablespoon Worcestershire sauce
- 1 teaspoon salt

- 1 tablespoon onion flakes
- Half soup can water
- ¼ teaspoon salt
- ⅛ teaspoon pepper

1. Combine all meat loaf ingredients. Shape into either a round or an oval loaf, to fit the shape of your crock pot, and place in greased cooker. 2. Cover. Cook on high 1 hour. 3. Combine sauce ingredients. Pour over meat loaf. 4. Cover. Cook on low 6 hours.

Barbecued Pot Roast

Prep time: 5 minutes | Cook time: 5 to 6 hours | Serves 10

- 1 (5-pound / 2.3-kg) roast
- 1 (16-ounce / 454-g) bottle honey barbecue sauce
- 1 small onion, chopped
- 1 clove garlic, minced
- Black pepper (optional)
- Montreal seasoning (optional)

1. Place the roast into the slow cooker. 2. Pour barbecue sauce over the top, ensuring it is well covered. 3. Sprinkle the chopped onion over the roast and place the garlic alongside it. 4. If desired, add a sprinkle of pepper and/or Montreal seasoning for extra flavor. 5. Cover the slow cooker and set it to cook on low for 5 to 6 hours. 6. After cooking, carefully remove the roast from the cooker and let it rest for 10 minutes before slicing. Serve with the cooking juices for added flavor.

Slow-Cooked Stuffed Green Peppers with Beef and Rice

Prep time: 40 minutes | Cook time: 5 to 7 hours | Serves 6

- 6 green peppers
- 1 pound (454 g) ground beef
- ¼ cup chopped onions
- 1 teaspoon salt
- ¼ teaspoon pepper
- 1¼ cups rice, cooked
- 1 tablespoon Worcestershire sauce
- 1 (8-ounce / 227-g) can tomato sauce
- ¼ cup beef broth

1. Cut stem ends from peppers. Carefully remove seeds and membrane without breaking pepper apart. Parboil in water for 5 minutes. Drain. Set aside. 2. Brown ground beef and onions in skillet. Drain off drippings. Place meat and onions in mixing bowl. 3. Add seasonings, rice, and Worcestershire sauce to meat and combine well. Stuff green peppers with mixture. Stand stuffed peppers upright in large crock pot. 4. Mix together tomato sauce and beef broth. Pour over peppers. 5. Cover. Cook on low 5 to 7 hours.

Veal Chops Braised in White Wine and Sage

Prep time: 20 minutes | Cook time: 5 to 6 hours | Serves 6

- 1½ teaspoons salt
- ½ teaspoon freshly ground black pepper
- 3 cloves garlic, minced
- 1 tablespoon finely chopped dried sage leaves
- 3 tablespoons extra-virgin olive oil
- 6 veal chops, 1 to 1½ inches thick
- 1 cup dry white wine or vermouth
- 1 (15-ounce / 425-g) can crushed plum tomatoes, with their juice
- ¼ cup balsamic vinegar
- ½ cup golden raisins

1. In a small bowl, create a paste by combining the salt, pepper, garlic, sage, and 1 tablespoon of oil. Rub this mixture evenly over the pork chops. In a large skillet, heat the remaining 2 tablespoons of oil over high heat. Add the chops in batches and brown them on both sides. 2. Once browned, transfer the chops to the insert of a 5- to 7-quart slow cooker. Depending on the size of your pot, you may need to stack the chops in two layers. 3. Pour the wine into the same skillet, allowing some of it to evaporate. Add the tomatoes and scrape any browned bits from the bottom of the pan, then transfer this mixture to the slow cooker. 4. Stir in the vinegar and raisins, mixing well to combine. 5. Cover the slow cooker and set it to cook on low for 5 to 6 hours, until the chops are tender. When

done, carefully remove the chops from the sauce and place them on a platter, covering them with aluminum foil. Pour the sauce into a small saucepan, bring it to a boil, and continue boiling until the sauce is reduced and concentrated. 6. Taste the sauce and adjust the seasoning as needed. Serve the chops drizzled with some of the sauce, and offer additional sauce on the side.

Slow-Cooked Lamb Shanks in Marsala Wine

Prep time: 15 minutes | Cook time: 9 hours | Serves 2

- 2 tablespoons extra-virgin olive oil
- 2 lamb shanks, trimmed and cracked
- ½ teaspoon salt
- ⅛ teaspoon freshly ground black pepper
- ½ cup chicken stock
- 1 leek, white part only,
- chopped
- 2 carrots, sliced
- 2 garlic cloves, minced
- 1 (14 ounces / 397 g) can diced tomatoes, undrained
- 1 cup Marsala wine
- 2 teaspoons minced fresh rosemary leaves

1. In a large saucepan over medium heat, heat the oil. 2. Sprinkle the lamb with the salt and pepper, add it to the pan, and brown it on all sides, turning several times, about 5 minutes. 3. Remove the lamb from the saucepan to a platter, and add the stock to the pan. Bring the stock to a simmer, scraping up the pan drippings. Remove from the heat. 4. In the crock pot, combine the leek, carrots, garlic, and tomatoes. Top with the lamb shanks, and pour the stock mixture from the saucepan over everything. 5. Add the wine and rosemary to the crock pot. 6. Cover and cook on low for 8 to 9 hours, or until the lamb is very tender, and serve.

Onion-Mushroom Pot Roast

Prep time: 10 minutes | Cook time: 5 to 12 hours | Serves 6

- 1 (3- to 4-pound / 1.4- to 1.8-kg) pot roast or chuck roast
- 1 (4-ounce / 113-g) can sliced mushrooms, drained
- 1 teaspoon salt
- ¼ teaspoon pepper
- ½ cup beef broth
- 1 envelope dry onion soup mix

1. Begin by placing the pot roast in the crock pot. 2. Add the mushrooms, along with salt and pepper, over the roast. 3. In a small bowl, combine the beef broth with the onion soup mix, then spoon this mixture over the roast. Cover the crock pot and cook on high for 5 to 6 hours or on low for 10 to 12 hours, until the meat is tender but remains moist.

Creamy Ham and Cheese Noodle Bake

Prep time: 30 minutes | Cook time: 2 to 4 hours | Serves 8 to 10

- 1 (16-ounce / 454-g) package medium egg noodles, divided
- 1 (10¾-ounce / 305-g) can condensed cream of celery soup
- 1 pint sour cream
- 2 cups fully cooked ham, cubed, divided
- 2 cups shredded cheese, your choice, divided

1. Prepare noodles according to package instructions. Drain. 2. In a small bowl combine soup and sour cream until smooth. Set aside. 3. In a greased crock pot, layer one-third of the cooked noodles, one-third of the ham, and one-third of the cheese. 4. Top with one-fourth of soup mixture. 5. Repeat steps 3 and 4 twice until all ingredients are used. The final layer should be the soup-sour cream mixture. 6. Cook 2 to 4 hours on low, or until heated through.

Mutton Cooked with Spices and Ground Lamb

Prep time: 15 minutes | Cook time: 6 to 8 hours | Serves 6 to 8

- 3 teaspoons rapeseed oil
- 2¾-inch piece cassia bark
- 2 black cardamom pods
- 6 green cardamom pods
- 10 black peppercorns
- 4 cloves
- 2 star anise
- 2 bay leaves
- 1 teaspoon cumin seeds
- 4 onions, finely chopped
- 8 garlic cloves, minced
- 8 dried red Kashmiri chiles
- 4 to 5 tomatoes, finely chopped
- 1 tablespoon freshly grated ginger
- 1 teaspoon turmeric
- 2 teaspoons coriander seeds, ground
- 1 teaspoon sea salt
- 14 ounces (397 g) ground mutton or lamb
- 1¾ pounds (794 g) mutton or lamb chunks (preferably on the bone)
- 1 teaspoon garam masala
- Handful fresh coriander leaves, chopped

1. In a frying pan (or in the crock pot if it has a sear setting), heat the oil and toast the cassia bark, black and green cardamom pods, peppercorns, cloves, star anise, bay leaves, and cumin seeds until they become fragrant, about 1 minute. Then add the onions and garlic, cooking for 5 to 10 minutes until they are soft and just beginning to brown. 2. While the onions are cooking, soak the chiles in boiling water for a few minutes to soften them, then drain.

3. In the crock pot, add the tomatoes, ginger, turmeric, ground coriander, salt, and the soaked chiles. 4. Incorporate the ground lamb into the mixture, using a wooden spoon to break it up and coat it in the sauce. 5. Stir in the pieces of mutton and mix everything thoroughly to ensure the meat begins to heat through. 6. Cover the crock pot and cook on low for 8 hours or on high for 6 hours. 7. Once the meat is tender and fully cooked, switch the crock pot to sauté or high and remove the lid to allow the sauce to reduce and thicken. If there's excess oil from the meat, skim it off with a ladle before proceeding. Cook for an additional 5 to 6 minutes. 8. Turn off the cooker and stir in the garam masala. Taste the dish and adjust the seasoning if needed. 9. Garnish with fresh coriander leaves and serve hot.

Cheesy Noodle Hamburger Casserole

Prep time: 20 minutes | Cook time: 3 to 4 hours | Serves 10

- 1½ pounds (680 g) ground beef, browned and drained
- 1 green pepper, diced
- 1 quart whole tomatoes
- 1 (10¾-ounce / 305-g) can cream of mushroom soup
- 1 large onion, diced
- 1½ tablespoons Worcestershire sauce
- 1 (8-ounce / 227-g) package noodles, uncooked
- 1 teaspoon salt
- ¼ teaspoon pepper
- 1 cup shredded cheese

1. Combine all ingredients except cheese in crock pot. 2. Cover. Cook on high 3 to 4 hours. 3. Sprinkle with cheese before serving.

Beef-Vegetable Casserole

Prep time: 20 minutes | Cook time: 4 to 5 hours | Serves 8

- 1 pound (454 g) extra-lean ground beef or turkey
- 1 medium onion, chopped
- ½ cup chopped celery
- 4 cups chopped cabbage
- 2½ cups canned stewed tomatoes, slightly mashed
- 1 tablespoon flour
- 1 teaspoon salt
- 1 tablespoon sugar
- ¼ to ½ teaspoon black pepper, according to your taste preference

1. In a nonstick skillet, sauté the meat, onion, and celery until the meat is browned. 2. Transfer the mixture into the crock pot. 3. Layer the top with cabbage, tomatoes, flour, salt, sugar, and pepper in that order. 4. Cover the crock pot and cook on high for 4 to 5 hours.

Slow-Cooked Pork and Cabbage with Apples

Prep time: 10 minutes | Cook time: 5 to 6 hours | Serves 8

- 2 pounds (907 g) pork steaks, or chops, or shoulder
- ¾ cup chopped onions
- ¼ cup chopped fresh parsley, or 2 tablespoons dried parsley
- 4 cups shredded cabbage
- 1 teaspoon salt
- ⅛ teaspoon pepper
- ½ teaspoon caraway seeds
- ⅛ teaspoon allspice
- ½ cup beef broth
- 2 cooking apples, cored and sliced ¼-inch thick

1. Place pork in crock pot. Layer onions, parsley, and cabbage over pork. 2. Combine salt, pepper, caraway seeds, and allspice. Sprinkle over cabbage. Pour broth over cabbage. 3. Cover. Cook on low 5 to 6 hours. 4. Add apple slices 30 minutes before serving.

Moroccan Meatballs in Spicy Tomato Sauce

Prep time: 20 minutes | Cook time: 6 hours | Serves 6

Moroccan Meatballs:
- ½ cup bread crumbs
- ¼ cup dried currants
- ½ yellow onion, finely chopped
- ½ teaspoon sea salt
- ½ teaspoon ground cumin

Spicy Tomato Sauce:
- ¼ cup tomato paste
- 1 teaspoon fennel seeds
- 1 teaspoon orange zest
- ½ teaspoon ground cumin
- ¼ teaspoon ground cinnamon
- ¼ teaspoon sea salt
- ¼ teaspoon ground red pepper

- ½ teaspoon dried oregano
- ¼ teaspoon ground cinnamon
- 1½ pounds (680 g) lean ground beef
- 1 large egg white

- 1 (28-ounce / 794-g) can whole tomatoes, coarsely chopped, with the juice
- 3 cups hot cooked couscous, for serving
- 2 tablespoons fresh chopped parsley, for serving (optional)

Make the Meatballs:

1. In a medium bowl, mix together the bread crumbs, currants, onion, salt, cumin, oregano, cinnamon, ground beef, and egg white until well combined. Form the mixture into 30 meatballs and place them on a plate. 2. Heat a large nonstick skillet over medium-high heat. Add half of the meatballs to the skillet and cook for about 3 minutes, or until browned, turning them frequently. Once browned, transfer the meatballs to the crock pot. Repeat this process with the remaining 15 meatballs.

Prepare the Sauce:

3. In another medium bowl, combine the tomato paste, fennel seeds, orange zest, cumin, cinnamon, salt, red pepper flakes, and tomatoes, mixing well. Pour this sauce over the meatballs in the crock pot, stirring gently to ensure the meatballs are coated with the sauce. 4. Cover the slow cooker and set it to low, cooking for 6 hours. 5. Serve the meatballs over couscous and garnish with parsley if desired.

Quick and Simple Crock Pot Meat Loaf

Prep time: 5 minutes | Cook time: 2 hours | Serves 5 to 6

- 2 pounds (907 g) ground beef
- 1 (6¼-ounce / 177-g) package stuffing mix for
- beef, plus seasoning
- 2 eggs, beaten
- ½ cup ketchup, divided

1. Mix beef, dry stuffing, eggs, and ¼ cup ketchup. 2. Shape into an oval loaf. Place in crock pot. Pour remaining ketchup over top. 3. Cover and cook on high for 2 hours.

Slow-Cooked Mexican Casserole with Ground Beef and Cheddar

Prep time: 15 minutes | Cook time: 8 to 9 hours | Serves 8

- 1 pound (454 g) extra-lean ground beef
- 1 medium onion, chopped
- 1 small green bell pepper, chopped
- 1 (16-ounce / 454-g) can kidney beans, rinsed and drained
- 1 (14½-ounce / 411-g) can diced tomatoes, undrained
- 1 (8-ounce / 227-g) can tomato sauce
- ¼ cup water
- 1 envelope reduced-sodium taco seasoning
- 1 tablespoon chili powder
- 1⅓ cups instant rice, uncooked
- 1 cup low-fat Cheddar cheese

1. Brown ground beef and onion in nonstick skillet. 2. Combine all ingredients in crock pot except rice and cheese. 3. Cook on low 8 to 9 hours. 4. Stir in rice, cover, and cook until tender. 5. Sprinkle with cheese. Cover and cook until cheese is melted. Serve.

Slow-Cooked Pork Chops with Apple-Onion Medley

Prep time: 15 minutes | Cook time: 6 to 8 hours | Serves 2

- 1 apple, cored, peeled, and cut into 8 wedges
- 1 sweet onion, cut into thick rings
- 1 teaspoon fresh thyme
- ¼ teaspoon ground cinnamon
- ¼ cup apple cider
- 2 bone-in pork chops
- ⅛ teaspoon sea salt
- Freshly ground black pepper

1. Put the apple, onion, thyme, and cinnamon in the crock pot and stir to combine. Pour in the apple cider. 2. Season the pork chops with the salt and a few grinds of the black pepper. Set the chops atop the apple and onion mixture. 3. Cover and cook on low for 6 to 8 hours, until the apples and onion are very soft and the pork is cooked through.

Creamy Veal Paprikash with Bell Peppers

Prep time: 30 minutes | Cook time: 4½ to 5½ hours | Serves 6

- 5 strips thick-cut bacon, cut into ½-inch pieces
- ½ cup all-purpose flour
- 1 teaspoon salt
- ¼ teaspoon hot paprika
- 2½ pounds (1.1 kg) boneless veal shoulder or shank, cut into 1-inch pieces
- 3 tablespoons olive oil
- ¼ cup sweet paprika
- 1 teaspoon dried marjoram
- 1 teaspoon dried thyme
- 1 large green bell pepper,
- seeded and coarsely chopped
- 1 large red bell pepper, seeded and coarsely chopped
- 1 large yellow bell pepper, seeded and coarsely chopped
- 1 (15-ounce / 425-g) can crushed plum tomatoes, with their juice
- 1 cup chicken broth
- ½ cup beef broth
- 1 bay leaf
- 1 cup sour cream at room temperature

1. Cook the bacon in a large skillet until crisp and transfer it to the insert of a 5- to 7-quart crock pot. Remove all but 3 tablespoons of the drippings in the pan. 2. Mix the flour, salt, and hot paprika in a large zipper-top plastic bag. Add the veal to the flour mixture, toss to coat, and shake off the excess. Heat the bacon drippings over medium-high heat. 3. Add the veal a few pieces at a time and brown on all sides. 4. Transfer the browned veal to the slow-cooker insert. Add the oil to the skillet over medium-high heat. Stir in the sweet paprika, marjoram, thyme, and bell peppers and sauté until the bell peppers begin to soften, 4 to 5 minutes. 5. Add the tomatoes and

both broths to the skillet and scrape up any browned bits from the bottom of the pan. Transfer the contents of the skillet to the slow-cooker insert. Add the bay leaf and stir to combine the ingredients. 6. Cover the crock pot and cook on low for 4½ to 5½ hours. Remove the bay leaf. Taste the stew and adjust the seasonings. Stir in the sour cream and serve the stew immediately.

Rustic Italian Braised Beef

Prep time: 10 minutes | Cook time: 8 to 9 hours | Serves 8 to 10

- 1 (3- to 3½-pound / 1.4- to 1.6-kg) boneless rump roast
- ½ teaspoon salt
- ½ teaspoon garlic powder
- ¼ teaspoon pepper
- 1 (4½-ounce / 128-g) jar mushroom pieces, drained
- 1 medium onion, diced
- 1 (14-ounce / 397-g) jar spaghetti sauce
- ¼ to ½ cup beef broth

1. Cut roast in half. 2. Combine salt, garlic powder, and pepper. Rub over both halves of the roast. Place in crock pot. 3. Top with mushrooms and onions. 4. Combine spaghetti sauce and broth. Pour over roast. 5. Cover. Cook on low 8 to 9 hours. 6. Slice roast. Serve.

Flavor-Filled Pork and Sauerkraut

Prep time: 30 minutes | Cook time: 10 to 11 hours | Serves 10 to 15

- 1 (4- to 5-pound / 1.8- to 2.3-kg) lean pork loin roast
- 1 (1- to 2-pound / 454 to 907-g) bag sauerkraut, divided
- Half a small head of cabbage, thinly sliced, divided
- 1 large onion, thinly sliced,
- divided
- 1 apple, quartered, cored, and sliced, divided
- 1 teaspoon dill weed (optional)
- ½ cup brown sugar (optional)
- 1 cup water

1. In a heavy nonstick skillet, brown the roast for 10 minutes on all sides, then transfer it to the crock pot. 2. Layer half of the sauerkraut over the roast, followed by half of the cabbage, half of the onion, and half of the apple. 3. Repeat these layers with the remaining sauerkraut, cabbage, onion, and apple. 4. If using dill weed and brown sugar, mix them with the water in a bowl, then pour this mixture over the layered ingredients. Alternatively, you can simply pour water over the top. 5. Cover the crock pot and cook on high for 1 hour. Then, reduce the heat to low and continue cooking until the meat is tender, which will take about 9 to 10 hours.

Savory Spiced Lamb and Pumpkin Stew

Prep time: 15 minutes | Cook time: 8 hours | Serves 6

- ¼ cup extra-virgin olive oil
- 1½ pounds (680 g) lamb shoulder, cut into 1-inch chunks
- 1 sweet onion, chopped
- 1 tablespoon minced garlic
- 4 cups pumpkin, cut into 1-inch pieces
- 2 carrots, diced
- 1 (14½ ounces / 411 g) can diced tomatoes
- 3 cups beef broth
- 2 tablespoons ras el hanout
- 1 teaspoon hot chili powder
- 1 teaspoon salt
- 1 cup Greek yogurt

1. Lightly grease the crock pot insert with 1 tablespoon olive oil. 2. Place a large skillet over medium–high heat and add the remaining oil. 3. Brown the lamb for 6 minutes, then add the onion and garlic. 4. Sauté 3 minutes more, then transfer the lamb and vegetables to the insert. 5. Add the pumpkin, carrots, tomatoes, broth, ras el hanout, chili powder, and salt to the insert and stir to combine. 6. Cover and cook on low for 8 hours 7. Serve topped with yogurt.

Guinness Corned Beef and Cabbage

Prep time: 20 minutes | Cook time: 8 hours | Serves 9

- 2 pounds (907 g) red potatoes, quartered
- 1 pound (454 g) carrots, cut into 3-inch pieces
- 2 celery ribs, cut into 3-inch pieces
- 1 small onion, quartered
- 1 (3- to 3½-pound / 1.4- to 1.6-kg) corned beef brisket with spice packet
- 8 whole cloves
- 6 whole peppercorns
- 1 bay leaf
- 1 (12-ounce / 340-g) bottle Guinness stout or reduced-sodium beef broth
- ½ small head cabbage, thinly sliced
- Prepared horseradish

1. In a 6-quart crock pot, combine the potatoes, carrots, celery, and onion. Place the corned beef on top (discard the spice packet or save it for another use). 2. In a double layer of cheesecloth, place the cloves, peppercorns, and bay leaf. Gather the corners of the cloth to enclose the seasonings and tie it securely with string. Add this spice bag to the crock pot and pour the stout over everything. 3. Cover the crock pot and cook on low for 8 to 10 hours, or until the meat and vegetables are tender. Add the cabbage during the last hour of cooking, then discard the spice bag before serving. 4. Slice the beef diagonally against the grain into thin pieces. Serve the beef alongside the vegetables and a side of horseradish for added flavor.

Saucy Pork Chops

Prep time: 15 minutes | Cook time: 6 to 8 hours | Serves 5

- 5 to 6 center-cut loin pork chops
- 3 tablespoons oil
- 1 onion, sliced
- 1 green pepper, cut in strips
- 1 (8-ounce / 227-g) can tomato sauce
- 3 to 4 tablespoons brown sugar
- 1 tablespoon vinegar
- 1½ teaspoons salt
- 1 to 2 teaspoons Worcestershire sauce

1. In a skillet, brown the chops in oil over medium heat, then transfer them to the crock pot. 2. Add the remaining ingredients to the slow cooker, mixing them together. 3. Cover the crock pot and set it to cook on low for 6 to 8 hours. 4. Once done, serve the chops hot.

Lemon Pork

Prep time: 15 minutes | Cook time: 7 to 8 hours | Serves 6

- 3 tablespoons extra-virgin olive oil, divided
- 1 tablespoon butter
- 2 pounds (907 g) pork loin roast
- ½ teaspoon salt
- ¼ teaspoon freshly ground
- black pepper
- ¼ cup chicken broth
- Juice and zest of 1 lemon
- 1 tablespoon minced garlic
- ½ cup heavy (whipping) cream

1. Begin by lightly greasing the insert of the crock pot with 1 tablespoon of olive oil. 2. In a large skillet over medium-high heat, combine the remaining 2 tablespoons of olive oil with the butter and heat until melted. 3. Season the pork lightly with salt and pepper, then add it to the skillet, browning the roast on all sides for about 10 minutes. Transfer the browned roast to the crock pot insert. 4. In a small bowl, mix together the broth, lemon juice, lemon zest, and garlic until well combined. 5. Pour the broth mixture over the roast in the crock pot. 6. Cover the crock pot and cook on low for 7 to 8 hours. 7. Once cooked, stir in the heavy cream and serve the dish warm.

Chili Cheese Bandito Dogs

Prep time: 10 minutes | Cook time: 3 to 3½ hours | Serves 10

- 1 pound (454 g) hot dogs
- 2 (15-ounce / 425-g) cans chili, with or without beans
- 1 (10¾-ounce / 305-g) can condensed Cheddar cheese soup
- 1 (4-ounce / 113-g) can chopped green chilies
- 10 hot dog buns
- 1 medium onion, chopped
- 1 to 2 cups corn chips, coarsely crushed
- 1 cup shredded Cheddar cheese

1. Place hot dogs in crock pot. 2. Combine chili, soup, and green chilies. Pour over hot dogs. 3. Cover. Cook on low 3 to 3½ hours. 4. Serve hot dogs in buns. Top with chili mixture, onion, corn chips, and cheese.

crock pot Enchiladas

Prep time: 30 minutes | Cook time: 5 to 7 hours | Serves 6

- 1 pound (454 g) lean ground beef
- 1 cup onions, chopped
- ½ cup green bell pepper, chopped
- 1 (16-ounce / 454-g) can pinto or kidney beans, rinsed and drained
- 1 (10-ounce / 283-g) can diced tomatoes and green chilies
- 1 cup water
- 1 teaspoon chili powder
- 1 (16-ounce / 454-g) can black beans, rinsed and drained
- ½ teaspoon ground cumin
- ½ teaspoon salt
- ¼ teaspoon black pepper
- Dash of dried red pepper flakes and/or several drops Tabasco sauce (optional)
- 1 cup shredded low-fat sharp Cheddar cheese
- 1 cup shredded low-fat Monterey Jack cheese
- 6 flour tortillas (6 or 7 inches)

1. In a nonstick skillet, brown the beef along with the onions and green pepper. 2. Add the remaining ingredients (excluding the cheeses and tortillas) to the skillet and bring the mixture to a boil. 3. Once boiling, reduce the heat, cover, and let it simmer for 10 minutes. 4. In a separate bowl, combine the cheeses. 5. In the crock pot, layer about ¾ cup of the beef mixture, followed by one tortilla, and then about ¼ cup of cheese. Continue to repeat these layers until all ingredients are used up. 6. Cover the crock pot and cook on low for 5 to 7 hours.

Pecos River Red-Frito Pie

Prep time: 10 minutes | Cook time: 8 to 10 hours | Serves 6

- 1 large onion, chopped coarsely
- 3 pounds (1.4 kg) coarsely ground hamburger
- 2 garlic cloves, minced
- 3 tablespoons ground hot red chili peppers
- 2 tablespoons ground mild red chili peppers
- 1½ cups water
- Corn chips
- Shredded Monterey Jack cheese
- Shredded Cheddar cheese

1. In the crock pot, combine the onion, hamburger, garlic, chilies, and water, mixing well. 2. Cover the crock pot and cook on low for 8 to 10 hours. Once cooked, drain any excess liquid. 3. Serve the mixture over corn chips and top with a blend of Monterey Jack and Cheddar cheeses for added flavor.

Bavarian Beef

Prep time: 15 minutes | Cook time: 6½ to 7½ hours | Serves 6

- 1 (3- to 3½-pound / 1.4- to 1.6-kg) boneless beef chuck roast
- Oil
- 3 cups sliced carrots
- 3 cups sliced onions
- 2 large kosher dill pickles, chopped
- 1 cup sliced celery
- ½ cup dry red wine or beef broth
- ⅓ cup German-style mustard
- 2 teaspoons coarsely ground black pepper
- 2 bay leaves
- ¼ teaspoon ground cloves
- 1 cup water
- ⅓ cup flour

1. In a skillet, brown the roast on both sides in oil, then transfer it to the crock pot. 2. Add the remaining ingredients to the slow cooker. 3. Cover the crock pot and cook on low for 6 to 7 hours. 4. Once cooked, remove the meat and vegetables to a large platter and cover to keep warm. 5. In a bowl, mix the flour with 1 cup of broth until smooth, then return this mixture to the cooker. Turn the heat to high and stir, cooking until the broth is smooth and thickened. 6. Serve the dish hot.

Meat Loaf and Mexico

Prep time: 15 minutes | Cook time: 4 to 4½ hours | Serves 6

- 1¼ pounds (567 g) extra-lean ground beef
- 4 cups hash browns, thawed
- 1 egg, lightly beaten, or egg substitute
- 2 tablespoons dry vegetable soup mix
- 2 tablespoons low-sodium taco seasoning
- 2 cups fat-free shredded Cheddar cheese, divided
- Nonfat cooking spray

1. In a mixing bowl, combine the ground beef, hash browns, egg, soup mix, taco seasoning, and 1 cup of cheese, mixing until well combined. Shape the mixture into a loaf. 2. Line the crock pot with aluminum foil, leaving enough overhang to use as handles for lifting the loaf out later. Spray the foil with nonstick cooking spray to prevent sticking. 3. Carefully place the loaf into the lined crock pot. Cover with the lid and cook on low for 4 hours. 4. After cooking, sprinkle the remaining cheese over the top of the loaf and cover again until the cheese is melted. 5. Using the foil handles, gently lift the loaf out of the crock pot and let it rest for 10 minutes before slicing and serving.

Chapter **5**

Fish and Seafood

Chapter 5 Fish and Seafood

Simple Poached Turbot

Prep time: 10 minutes | Cook time: 40 to 50 minutes | Serves 4

- 1 cup vegetable or chicken stock
- ½ cup dry white wine
- 1 yellow onion, sliced
- 1 lemon, sliced
- 4 sprigs fresh dill
- ½ teaspoon sea salt
- 4 (6-ounce / 170-g) turbot fillets

1. In the crock pot, combine the stock and wine. Cover and heat on high for 20 to 30 minutes to warm the liquid. 2. Once heated, add the chopped onion, lemon slices, dill, salt, and turbot to the crock pot. Cover again and cook on high for approximately 20 minutes, or until the turbot is opaque and cooked to your preference. 3. Serve the dish hot and enjoy!

Scallop and Crab Cioppino

Prep time: 15 minutes | Cook time: 7 hours | Serves 4

- Cooking oil spray
- 1 medium yellow onion, finely chopped
- 4 cloves garlic, minced
- 1 (15-ounce / 425-g) can diced tomatoes, with the juice
- 1 (10-ounce / 283-g) can diced tomatoes with green chiles
- 2 cups seafood stock
- 1 cup red wine
- 3 tablespoons chopped fresh basil
- 2 bay leaves
- 1 pound (454 g) cooked crab meat, shredded
- 1½ pounds (680 g) scallops
- Sea salt
- Black pepper
- ¼ cup fresh flat-leaf parsley, for garnish

1. Spray a large sauté pan with cooking oil and heat it over medium-high heat. Add the onion and sauté for about 5 minutes until it becomes softened. 2. Stir in the garlic and continue to sauté until it turns golden and fragrant, approximately 2 minutes. 3. Transfer the sautéed onion and garlic to the crock pot, then add the tomatoes, tomatoes with green chiles, stock, wine, basil, and bay leaves. Cover the crock pot and cook on low for 6 hours. 4.

About 30 minutes before the cooking time is finished, add the crab meat and scallops to the crock pot. Cover and cook on high for 30 minutes, or until the seafood turns opaque. Season with salt and pepper to taste. Serve hot, garnished with parsley.

Mahi-Mahi with Pineapple-Mango-Strawberry Salsa and Lentils

Prep time: 30 minutes | Cook time: 6 hours | Serves 6

- 1¼ cups vegetable or chicken stock
- 1 cup orange juice
- ¾ cup orange lentils
- ½ cup finely diced carrot
- ¼ cup finely diced red onion
- ¼ cup finely diced celery

Salsa:

- ¾ cup finely diced pineapple
- ¾ cup finely diced mango
- ½ cup finely diced strawberries
- ¼ cup finely diced red onion
- 1 tablespoon honey
- 6 (4- to-5-ounce / 113- to 142-g) mahi-mahi fillets
- Sea salt
- Black pepper
- 1 teaspoon lemon juice

- 2 tablespoons chopped fresh mint (or 2 teaspoons dried)
- 2 tablespoons orange juice
- 1 tablespoon lime juice
- ¼ teaspoon salt

1. In the crock pot, combine the stock, orange juice, lentils, carrot, onion, celery, and honey, stirring to mix well. 2. Cover the pot and cook on low for 5 to 5½ hours, or until the lentils are tender. 3. Once the lentils are cooked, place a sheet of parchment paper over them. Lightly season the mahi-mahi with salt and black pepper, then place it on the parchment (skin-side down, if the skin is intact). Cover the pot again and continue cooking on low for an additional 25 minutes, or until the mahi-mahi is opaque in the center. To remove the fish, lift out the parchment paper and transfer it to a plate. 4. Stir the lemon juice into the lentils and season with additional salt and pepper to taste.

Make the Salsa:

5. While the fish is cooking, combine the pineapple, mango, strawberries, red onion, mint, orange juice, lime juice, and salt in a large jar. Mix well and chill to allow the flavors to meld. 6. To serve, place about ½ cup of hot lentils on a plate, top with a mahi-mahi fillet, and add ⅓ cup of salsa on top.

Mediterranean Fisherman's Stew

Prep time: 20 minutes | Cook time: 7 hours | Serves 6 to 8

◆ ½ cup extra-virgin olive oil	◆ 1 (28- to 32-ounce / 794- to 907-g) can crushed tomatoes
◆ 2 medium onions, finely chopped	◆ 2 cups clam juice
◆ 2 medium red bell peppers, seeded and finely chopped	◆ 1 cup chicken broth
◆ 6 cloves garlic, minced	◆ 2 pounds (907 g) firm-fleshed fish, such as halibut, monkfish, cod, or sea bass fillets, cut into 1-inch chunks
◆ 1 teaspoon saffron threads, crushed	
◆ 1 teaspoon hot paprika	◆ 1½ pounds (680 g) littleneck clams
◆ 1 cup finely chopped Spanish chorizo or soppressata salami	◆ ½ cup finely chopped fresh Italian parsley

1. Heat the oil in a large skillet over medium-high heat. Add the onions, bell peppers, garlic, saffron, paprika, and chorizo and sauté until the vegetables are softened, 5 to 7 minutes. Add the tomatoes and transfer the contents of the skillet to the insert of a 5- to 7-quart crock pot. Add the clam juice and broth and stir to combine. 2. Cover and cook on low for 6 hours. Add the fish and clams to the slow-cooker insert, spooning some of the sauce over the fish and pushing the clams under the sauce. 3. Cover and cook for an additional 45 to 50 minutes, until the clams have opened and the fish is cooked through and opaque. Discard any clams that haven't opened. 4. Sprinkle the parsley over the stew and serve immediately.

Lemon-Butter Potato Crusted Sea Bass

Prep time: 15 minutes | Cook time: 1½ hours | Serves 6

◆ 1 cup (2 sticks) unsalted butter, melted and cooled	seasoning
◆ ½ cup fresh lemon juice	◆ 2 to 3 pounds (907 g to 1.4 kg) sea bass fillets, cut to fit the slow-cooker insert
◆ Grated zest of 1 lemon	
◆ 2 cloves garlic, minced	◆ 6 medium Yukon gold potatoes, cut into ¼-inch-thick slices
◆ 8 tablespoons olive oil	
◆ 2 tablespoons Old Bay	

1. Stir the butter, lemon juice, zest, garlic, and 2 tablespoons of the olive oil together in a small bowl. Combine the remaining 6 tablespoons oil and the seasoning in a large mixing bowl. 2. Paint the sea bass with some of the butter sauce and set aside. Toss the potatoes in the seasoned oil. Pour half the butter sauce in the insert of a 5- to 7-quart crock pot. 3. Place half the potatoes in the bottom of the crock pot. Place the sea bass on top of the potatoes and pour half the remaining butter sauce over the sea bass. Place the remaining potatoes on top of the sea bass and drizzle with the remaining butter sauce. 4. Cover and cook on high for 1½ hours, until the potatoes begin to turn golden and the sea bass is cooked through and opaque in the middle. Remove the cover and cook for an additional 15 to 20 minutes. 5. Serve immediately.

Moroccan Sea Bass

Prep time: 20 minutes | Cook time: 3 to 4 hours | Serves 8

◆ 2 tablespoons extra-virgin olive oil	◆ ½ teaspoon ground ginger
◆ 1 large yellow onion, finely chopped	◆ 1 (15-ounce / 425-g) can diced tomatoes, with the juice
◆ 1 medium red bell pepper, cut into ½-inch strips	◆ ¼ cup fresh orange juice
◆ 1 medium yellow bell pepper, cut into ½-inch strips	◆ 2 pounds (907 g) fresh sea bass fillets
◆ 4 garlic cloves, minced	◆ ¼ cup finely chopped fresh flat-leaf parsley
◆ 1 teaspoon saffron threads, crushed in the palm of your hand	◆ ¼ cup finely chopped fresh cilantro
◆ 1½ teaspoons sweet paprika	◆ Sea salt
◆ ¼ teaspoon hot paprika or ¼ teaspoon smoked paprika (or pimentón)	◆ Black pepper
	◆ 1 navel orange, thinly sliced, for garnish

1. Begin by heating olive oil in a large skillet over medium-high heat. Add the diced onion along with the chopped red and yellow bell peppers, minced garlic, saffron strands, sweet paprika, and your choice of hot or smoked paprika, and grated ginger. Sauté the mixture for about 3 minutes, or until the onions start to become translucent. 2. Incorporate the diced tomatoes into the skillet, stirring for an additional 2 minutes to allow the flavors to meld together. 3. Transfer this flavorful blend to the crock pot and pour in the fresh orange juice, mixing well. 4. Arrange the sea bass fillets on top of the tomato sauce, ensuring they are well-covered with some of the mixture. Cover the crock pot and set it to cook on high for 2 hours, or on low for 3 to 4 hours, until the sea bass is fully cooked and opaque in the center. 5. Once the fish is ready, carefully remove it from the crock pot with a spatula and place it on a serving dish, covering it loosely with aluminum foil to keep it warm. 6. Remove any excess fat from the sauce, then mix in chopped parsley and cilantro, seasoning with salt and pepper to taste. 7. Drizzle some of the sauce over the sea bass and garnish with fresh orange slices for an extra touch. Serve the dish hot, along with the remaining sauce on the side for drizzling.

Cajun Shrimp

Prep time: 15 minutes | Cook time: 3½ to 7 hours | Serves 6

¾ pound (340 g) andouille sausage, cut into ½-inch rounds (you may substitute Kiel-basa if you cannot find andouille sausage)	2 tablespoons all-purpose flour
	1 (28-ounce / 794-g) can diced tomatoes, with their juice
1 red onion, sliced into wedges	¼ teaspoon cayenne pepper
2 garlic cloves, minced	Coarse sea salt
2 celery stalks, coarsely chopped	½ pound (227 g) large shrimp, peeled and deveined
1 red or green bell pepper, coarsely chopped	2 cups fresh okra, sliced (you may substitute frozen and thawed, if necessary)

1. In the crock pot, combine the sausage, onion, garlic, celery, and bell pepper. Sprinkle the mixture with flour and toss well to coat all the ingredients evenly. 2. Add the tomatoes and ½ cup of water to the pot. Season with cayenne pepper and salt to taste. 3. Cover the crock pot and cook on high for 3½ hours or on low for 7 hours, until the vegetables have softened. 4. Once the vegetables are tender, stir in the shrimp and okra. Cover again and cook until the shrimp turn opaque throughout, which will take about 30 minutes on high or 1 hour on low. Serve hot and enjoy!

Fiery Tomato Basil Mussels

Prep time: 15 minutes | Cook time: 7 hours | Serves 4

3 tablespoons olive oil	¾ cup white wine
4 cloves garlic, minced	2 tablespoons dried oregano
3 shallot cloves, minced	½ tablespoon dried basil
8 ounces (227 g) mushrooms, diced	½ teaspoon black pepper
	1 teaspoon paprika
1 (28-ounce / 794-g) can diced tomatoes, with the juice	¼ teaspoon red pepper flakes
	3 pounds (1.4 kg) mussels

1. In a large sauté pan, heat the olive oil over medium-high heat. Cook the garlic, shallots, and mushrooms for 2 to 3 minutes, until the garlic is just a bit brown and fragrant. Scrape the entire contents of the pan into the crock pot. 2. Add the tomatoes and white wine to the crock pot. Sprinkle with the oregano, basil, black pepper, paprika, and red pepper flakes. 3. Cover and cook on low for 4 to 5 hours, or on high for 2 to 3 hours. The mixture is done cooking when mushrooms are fork tender. 4. Clean and debeard the mussels.

Discard any open mussels. 5. Increase the heat on the crock pot to high once the mushroom mixture is done. Add the cleaned mussels to the crock pot and secure the lid tightly. Cook for 30 more minutes. 6. To serve, ladle the mussels into bowls with plenty of broth. Discard any mussels that didn't open up during cooking. Serve hot, with crusty bread for sopping up the sauce.

Creole Crayfish

Prep time: 15 minutes | Cook time: 3 to 8 hours | Serves 2

1½ cups diced celery	with the juice
1 large yellow onion, chopped	1 clove garlic, minced
2 small bell peppers, any colors, chopped	1 teaspoon sea salt
	¼ teaspoon black pepper
1 (8-ounce / 227-g) can tomato sauce	6 drops hot pepper sauce (like Tabasco)
1 (28-ounce / 794-g) can whole tomatoes, broken up,	1 pound (454 g) precooked crayfish meat

1. In the crock pot, layer the celery, onion, and bell peppers. Pour in the tomato sauce, diced tomatoes, and minced garlic. Season with salt, pepper, and add the hot sauce to taste. 2. Cover the crock pot and set it to cook on high for 3 to 4 hours, or on low for 6 to 8 hours. 3. Approximately 30 minutes before the cooking time is finished, stir in the crayfish to heat through. 4. Serve the dish hot and enjoy!

Zesty Lime-Infused Salmon Packets

Prep time: 10 minutes | Cook time: 2 hours | Serves 2

2 (6-ounce / 170-g) salmon fillets	2 cloves garlic, minced
	1 teaspoon finely chopped fresh parsley
1 tablespoon olive oil	¼ teaspoon black pepper
½ tablespoon lime juice	

1. Spread a length of foil onto the countertop, and put the salmon fillets directly in the middle. 2. In a small bowl, combine the olive oil, lime juice, garlic, parsley, and black pepper. Brush the mixture over the fillets. Fold the foil over and crimp the sides to make a packet. 3. Place the packet into the crock pot. Cover and cook on high for 2 hours. 4. Salmon is finished when it flakes easily with a fork. Serve hot.

Citrus Swordfish

Prep time: 15 minutes | Cook time: 1½ hours | Serves 2

- Nonstick cooking oil spray
- 1½ pounds (680 g) swordfish fillets
- Sea salt
- Black pepper
- 1 yellow onion, chopped
- 5 tablespoons chopped fresh flat-leaf parsley
- 1 tablespoon olive oil
- 2 teaspoons lemon zest
- 2 teaspoons orange zest
- Orange and lemon slices, for garnish
- Fresh parsley sprigs, for garnish

1. Begin by spraying the interior of the crock pot with nonstick cooking oil spray to prevent sticking. 2. Season the fish fillets generously with salt and pepper, then place them in the crock pot. 3. Evenly distribute the chopped onion, parsley, olive oil, lemon zest, and orange zest over the fish fillets. 4. Cover the crock pot and set it to cook on low for 1½ hours, allowing the flavors to meld. 5. Once cooked, serve the fish hot, garnished with slices of orange and lemon, along with sprigs of fresh parsley for a vibrant presentation.

Sea Bass Tagine

Prep time: 25 minutes | Cook time: 6 to 7½ hours | Serves 6

- 2 pounds (907 g) sea bass fillets
- ½ cup olive oil
- Grated zest of 1 lemon
- ¼ cup lemon juice
- 1 teaspoon sweet paprika
- ½ cup finely chopped fresh cilantro
- 2 cloves garlic, chopped
- 1 medium onion, finely chopped
- 1 teaspoon ground cumin
- ½ teaspoon saffron threads, crushed
- 1 (28- to 32-ounce / 794- to 907-g) can crushed tomatoes, with their juice
- 6 medium Yukon gold potatoes, quartered
- 1 teaspoon salt
- ½ teaspoon freshly ground black pepper
- ½ cup finely chopped fresh Italian parsley

1. Start by placing the fish into a zipper-top plastic bag for marinating. 2. In a small bowl, whisk together ¼ cup of oil, lemon zest, lemon juice, paprika, and chopped cilantro until well combined. Pour this marinade over the fish in the bag, seal it tightly, and refrigerate for a minimum of 1 hour, or up to 4 hours to allow the flavors to meld. 3. In a large skillet, heat the remaining ¼ cup of oil over medium-high heat. Add the minced garlic, diced onion, cumin, and saffron, sautéing until the onion becomes soft, which should take about 5 to 7 minutes. 4. Stir in the chopped tomatoes and mix well. In the insert of a 5- to 7-quart crock pot, layer the potatoes at the bottom and season them with salt and pepper, tossing to ensure they are evenly coated. Pour the tomato mixture over the potatoes. Cover and cook on low for 5 to 6 hours, or until the potatoes are nearly tender. 5. After the cooking time, pour the marinade into the crock pot and gently stir to combine the potatoes and sauce. Place the marinated fish on top of the potatoes, spooning some sauce over the fish as well. Cook for an additional 1 to 1½ hours until the sea bass is fully cooked and opaque throughout. 6. Once ready, sprinkle fresh parsley over the top of the sea bass and serve immediately, ensuring to scoop some potatoes and sauce with each serving of fish.

Hearty Fisherman's Seafood Stew

Prep time: 15 minutes | Cook time: 6 hours | Serves 8

- 1 pound (454 g) waxy baby potatoes, such as Yukon Gold
- 2 medium onions, finely chopped
- 2 celery stalks, finely chopped
- 5 garlic cloves, minced
- 1 (28-ounce / 794-g) can crushed tomatoes
- 1 (8-ounce / 227-g) bottle clam juice
- 8 ounces (227 g) low-sodium fish stock
- 1 (6-ounce / 170-g) can tomato paste
- 1 tablespoon balsamic vinegar
- 1 teaspoon sugar
- ½ teaspoon celery salt
- ½ teaspoon kosher salt, plus more for seasoning
- ½ teaspoon freshly ground black pepper, plus more for seasoning
- 2 bay leaves
- 1 pound (454 g) firm-fleshed white fish, such as cod, cut into 1-inch pieces
- ½ pound (227 g) medium uncooked shrimp, shelled and deveined
- ½ pound (227 g) scallops, small side muscle removed, halved
- ¼ cup finely chopped flat-leaf parsley, for garnish

1. To the crock pot, add the potatoes, onions, celery, garlic, tomatoes, clam juice, fish stock, tomato paste, vinegar, sugar, celery salt, kosher salt, pepper, and bay leaves. Stir to combine. Cover and cook on low for 6 hours, or until the potatoes are tender when pierced with a fork. 2. About 30 minutes before serving, add the white fish, shrimp, and scallops. Cover and continue cooking on low until cooked through. 3. Discard the bay leaves. Season with additional salt and pepper, as needed. Ladle the stew into bowls, garnish with the parsley, and serve immediately.

Smoked Salmon and Potato Casserole

Prep time: 10 minutes | Cook time: 8 hours | Serves 2

- 1 teaspoon butter, at room temperature, or extra-virgin olive oil
- 2 eggs
- 1 cup 2% milk
- 1 teaspoon dried dill
- ⅛ teaspoon sea salt
- Freshly ground black pepper
- 2 medium russet potatoes, peeled and sliced thin
- 4 ounces (113 g) smoked salmon

1. Begin by greasing the interior of the crock pot with butter to prevent sticking. 2. In a small bowl, whisk together the eggs, milk, dill, salt, and a few grinds of black pepper until well combined. 3. Layer one-third of the sliced potatoes evenly across the bottom of the crock pot, then top with one-third of the salmon. Pour one-third of the egg mixture over the salmon. Repeat this process with the remaining potatoes, salmon, and egg mixture, creating a final layer on top. 4. Cover the crock pot and set it to cook on low for 8 hours or overnight for a delicious meal.

Fiery BBQ Seafood Medley

Prep time: 20 minutes | Cook time: 1 hour | Serves 2

- ½ teaspoon paprika
- ½ teaspoon garlic powder
- ¼ teaspoon onion powder
- ¼ teaspoon cayenne pepper
- ¼ teaspoon dried oregano
- ¼ teaspoon dried thyme
- ½ teaspoon sea salt
- ½ teaspoon black pepper
- 2 cloves garlic, minced
- ½ cup olive oil
- ¼ cup Worcestershire sauce
- 1 tablespoon hot pepper sauce (like Tabasco)
- Juice of 1 lemon
- 1 pound (454 g) scallops
- 1 pound (454 g) large shrimp, unpeeled
- 1 green onion, finely chopped

1. Combine the paprika, garlic powder, onion powder, cayenne pepper, oregano, thyme, ½ teaspoon salt, and ¼ teaspoon black pepper. 2. Combine the paprika blend, garlic, olive oil, Worcestershire sauce, hot pepper sauce, and lemon juice in the crock pot. Season with salt and pepper. 3. Cover and cook on high for 30 minutes or until hot. 4. Rinse the scallops and shrimp, and drain. 5. Spoon one-half of the sauce from the crock pot into a glass measuring cup. 6. Place the scallops and shrimp in the crock pot with the remaining sauce. Drizzle with the sauce in the measuring cup, and stir to coat. 7. Cover and cook on high for 30 minutes, until the scallops and shrimp are opaque. 8. Turn the heat to warm for serving. Sprinkle with the chopped green onion to serve.

Aromatic Coconut Seafood Laksa

Prep time: 30 minutes | Cook time: 2½ hours | Serves 6 to 8

- 2 tablespoons virgin coconut oil or extra-virgin olive oil
- 1 small onion, chopped
- 4 Thai bird chiles
- 1 (2-inch) piece fresh ginger, peeled and grated
- 1 (1-inch) piece fresh turmeric, peeled and grated
- 1 lemongrass stalk, tough outer leaves discarded, inner bulb chopped
- ¼ cup fresh cilantro
- 1 tablespoon tamarind paste
- ½ teaspoon ground cumin
- ½ teaspoon paprika
- 2 teaspoon coarse salt
- 2 cups unsweetened coconut milk
- 2 cups boiling water
- 4 kaffir lime leaves
- 2 teaspoon fish sauce
- 1 pound (454 g) medium shrimp, peeled and deveined (shells rinsed and reserved)
- 2 pounds (907 g) small mussels, scrubbed
- ¾ pound (340 g) firm fish fillet, such as halibut or cod, cut into 1-inch pieces
- 8 ounces (227 g) rice noodles
- Lime wedges, cubed firm tofu, sliced scallions, sliced Thai bird chiles, cilantro, and chili oil, for serving

1. Preheat a 7-quart crock pot. 2. Heat oil in a saucepan over medium. Add onion and cook until translucent, about 5 minutes. Add chiles, ginger, turmeric, lemongrass, cilantro, tamarind paste, cumin, paprika, and salt. Cook until fragrant, about 2 more minutes. Remove from heat and let cool. Transfer spice mixture to a food processor and puree to a thick paste. 3. Combine laksa paste, coconut milk, the boiling water, lime leaves, fish sauce, and shrimp shells in the crock pot. Cover and cook on low for 2 hours (we prefer this recipe on low). 4. Strain liquid through a medium sieve into a bowl, pressing down on solids; return broth to crock pot (discard solids). Add shrimp and mussels, and cook on low 20 minutes. Add fish and cook until shrimp is completely cooked through, fish is firm, and mussels open, about 10 minutes. 5. Meanwhile, prepare noodles according to package instructions. 6. To serve, divide noodles among bowls. Add broth and seafood, and top with tofu, scallions, chiles, and cilantro. Serve with lime wedges and chili oil.

Mediterranean Olive Oil Poached Tuna

Prep time: 5 minutes | Cook time: 3 to 4 hours | Serves 6

- 3 pounds (1.4 kg) tuna fillets
- Olive oil to cover the fish
- 1 teaspoon coarse sea salt

1. Place the tuna in the insert of a 5- to 7-quart crock pot and pour the oil over the tuna. The oil should cover the tuna, and depending on the shape of your crock pot, you may need to add a bit more oil. Add the salt to the slow-cooker insert. 2. Cover and cook on low for 3 to 4 hours, until the tuna is cooked through and is white. Remove the tuna from the oil and cool completely before using.

Poached Salmon Cakes in White Wine Butter Sauce

Prep time: 15 minutes | Cook time: 5 hours | Serves 6

White Wine Butter Sauce:
- ½ cup (1 stick) unsalted butter
- 1 teaspoon Old Bay seasoning
- 2 cloves garlic, sliced
- 2 ½ cups white wine or vermouth

Salmon Cakes:
- 4 cups cooked salmon, flaked
- 1 (6-ounce / 170-g) jar marinated artichoke hearts, drained and coarsely chopped
- 1 cup fresh bread crumbs
- ½ cup freshly grated Parmigiano-Reggiano cheese
- 1 large egg, beaten
- ½ teaspoon freshly ground black pepper

1. In the insert of a 5- to 7-quart crock pot, combine all the sauce ingredients and stir until well mixed. Cover the pot and cook on low for 4 hours. 2. In a large mixing bowl, combine all the ingredients for the salmon cakes and mix thoroughly. Shape the mixture into 2-inch cakes. Gently place the cakes into the simmering sauce and spoon some of the sauce over the top. 3. Cover the crock pot again and cook for an additional hour, or until the cakes are tender. Carefully transfer the cakes to a serving platter. 4. Strain the sauce through a fine-mesh sieve into a saucepan, discarding any solids.

Bring the sauce to a boil and let it reduce by half. 5. Serve the reduced sauce over the salmon cakes or on the side as a dipping sauce.

Herb-Crusted Mediterranean Cod Bake

Prep time: 20 minutes | Cook time: 1 hour | Serves 6

- 6 tablespoons olive oil
- 3 tablespoons all-purpose flour
- 1½ teaspoons sea salt
- ½ tablespoon dry mustard
- 1 teaspoon rosemary
- ¼ tablespoon ground nutmeg
- 1¼ cups milk
- 2 teaspoons lemon juice
- ⅓ cup grated Parmesan cheese
- ⅓ cup grated Asiago cheese
- ⅓ cup grated Romano cheese
- 3 pounds (1.4 kg) Pacific cod fillets

Make the Orange Layer: 1. Heat the olive oil in a small saucepan over medium heat. Stir in the flour, salt, mustard, rosemary, and nutmeg. 2. Gradually add the milk, stirring constantly until thickened. 3. Add the lemon juice, and the Parmesan, Asiago, and Romano cheeses to the saucepan. Stir until the cheeses are melted. 4. Place the fish into the crock pot, and spoon the cheese sauce over the fish. Cover and cook on high for 1 to 1½ hours or until the fish flakes. Serve hot.

Sweet & Zesty Dill Salmon

Prep time: 10 minutes | Cook time: 1½ hours | Serves 6

- 3 pounds (1.4 kg) salmon fillets
- ½ cup Colman's English mustard
- ¼ cup honey
- 2 tablespoons finely chopped fresh dill

1. Place the salmon in the insert of a 5- to 7-quart crock pot. Put the mustard, honey, and dill in a small bowl and stir to combine. 2. Pour the mixture over the salmon, spreading evenly. 3. Cover and cook on high for 1½ hours, until the salmon is cooked through. 4. Serve the salmon from the crock pot topped with some of the sauce.

Chapter **6**

Stews and Soups

Chapter 6 Stews and Soups

Creamy Turkey Potpie Soup

Prep time: 20 minutes | Cook time: 7 to 8 hours | Serves 8

- 1 tablespoon extra-virgin olive oil
- 4 cups chicken broth
- ½ pound (227 g) skinless turkey breast, cut into ½-inch chunks
- 2 celery stalks, chopped
- 1 carrot, diced
- 1 sweet onion, chopped
- 2 teaspoons minced garlic
- 2 teaspoons chopped fresh thyme
- 1 cup cream cheese, diced
- 2 cups heavy (whipping) cream
- 1 cup green beans, cut into 1-inch pieces
- Salt, for seasoning
- Freshly ground black pepper, for seasoning

1. Lightly grease the insert of the crock pot with the olive oil. 2. Place the broth, turkey, celery, carrot, onion, garlic, and thyme in the insert. 3. Cover and cook on low for 7 to 8 hours. 4. Stir in the cream cheese, heavy cream, and green beans. 5. Season with salt and pepper and serve.

Back Bay Corn Chowder

Prep time: 15 minutes | Cook time: 3½ to 7½ hours | Serves 8

- 8 strips bacon, cut into ½-inch dice
- 1 cup finely chopped onion
- 3 stalks celery, finely chopped
- 1½ teaspoons dried thyme leaves
- ½ cup all-purpose flour
- 4 cups chicken or vegetable broth
- Tabasco sauce
- 4 cups diced red potatoes
- 1 (16-ounce / 454-g) package frozen petite white corn, defrosted
- 1 cup heavy cream
- Salt

1. In a large skillet, cook the bacon over medium heat until it becomes crispy. Add the chopped onion, celery, and thyme, and continue to cook over medium-high heat until the onion starts to soften. Sprinkle in the flour and cook for about 3 minutes, stirring constantly. Gradually whisk in the broth and 8 drops of Tabasco, mixing until smooth, and bring the mixture to a boil. 2. Pour the contents of the skillet into the insert of a 5- to 7-quart crock pot. Add the diced potatoes and corn, stirring to combine. Cover the crock pot and set it to cook on high for 3 hours or on low for 6 to 7 hours. 3. When the cooking time is nearly complete, stir in the cream, re-cover the crock pot, and cook on low for an additional 30 minutes. Adjust the seasoning with salt and additional Tabasco to taste. 4. Serve the chowder hot, enjoying its rich and hearty flavors.

Mixed Shellfish Chowder

Prep time: 20 minutes | Cook time: 5 hours | Serves 8

- 4 tablespoons (½ stick) unsalted butter
- 1 medium onion, finely chopped
- 3 stalks celery, finely chopped
- 1 teaspoon sweet paprika
- ½ teaspoon dried thyme
- 3 tablespoons all-purpose flour
- 6 cups lobster stock
- 2 tablespoons brandy
- ½ pound (227 g) cooked lobster meat, picked over for shells and cartilage
- ½ pound (227 g) lump crab meat, picked over for shells and cartilage
- ¼ pound (113 g) bay or sea scallops, cut into quarters
- 1 cup heavy cream
- ¼ cup finely chopped fresh chives, for garnish

1. In a saucepan over medium-high heat, melt the butter. Add the chopped onion, celery, paprika, and thyme, sautéing until the vegetables begin to soften, which should take about 3 minutes. Whisk in the flour and continue cooking for 2 to 3 minutes, stirring constantly to create a roux. Gradually stir in the stock and brandy, bringing the mixture to a boil. 2. Transfer the contents of the saucepan into the insert of a 5- to 7-quart crock pot. Cover the pot and cook on low for 4 hours. After this time, add the lobster, crab, scallops, and cream, then cover and cook on low for an additional hour to allow the flavors to meld. 3. When ready to serve, ladle the soup into bowls and garnish with fresh chives for a delightful finish.

Saigon Chicken Rice Soup

Prep time: 15 minutes | Cook time: 6 hours | Serves 8

- 8 cups chicken broth
- 4 chicken breast halves, skin and bones removed
- 3 dime-size thin slices fresh ginger
- 1 tablespoon soy sauce
- 1 teaspoon Asian fish sauce
- 1 teaspoon chili garlic sauce
- ½ cup grated carrot
- 1 cup thinly sliced Napa cabbage
- 6 green onions, thinly sliced on a diagonal
- 2 cups cooked jasmine rice

1. Begin by pouring the broth into the insert of a 5- to 7-quart crock pot. 2. Place the chicken at the bottom of the slow cooker and add the ginger, soy sauce, fish sauce, and chili sauce on top of the chicken. Cover the pot and cook on high for 4 hours. 3. After 4 hours, strain the broth through a fine-mesh sieve into a bowl, and shred the chicken into bite-sized pieces. 4. Return the shredded chicken and strained broth to the slow cooker, then stir in the carrot, cabbage, green onions, and rice. Keep the mixture warm on low for up to 2 hours before serving. If the soup becomes too thick, simply add more broth to reach your desired consistency.

Southwestern Flavor Burst Soup

Prep time: 15 minutes | Cook time: 6 to 8 hours | Serves 4

- 2 (14-ounce / 397-g) cans beef broth
- ½ cup sliced carrots
- ½ cup diced onions
- 1 cup diced potatoes
- 1 garlic clove, minced

Garnishes:
- Shredded cheese
- Diced avocados
- Diced green peppers
- Diced cucumbers
- 1 (6-ounce / 170-g) can cooked and peeled tiny

- 1 (8-ounce / 227-g) can or 1 cup home-canned crushed tomatoes
- 1 tablespoon Worcestershire sauce
- Salsa to taste

shrimp
- 1 cup cooked ham, diced
- 1 cup sliced green onion
- 3 hard-cooked eggs, chopped
- 1 cup diced tomatoes
- Sour cream

1. Combine broth, carrots, onions, potatoes, garlic, tomatoes, and Worcestershire sauce in crock pot. Cook on low 6 to 8 hours. 2. Before serving, stir in salsa, sampling as you go to get the right balance of flavors. 3. Serve the soup in bowls. Offer your choice of garnishes as toppings.

Grace's Hearty Minestrone

Prep time: 15 minutes | Cook time: 8 hours | Serves 8

- ¾ cup dry elbow macaroni
- 2 quarts chicken stock
- 2 large onions, diced
- 2 carrots, sliced
- Half a head of cabbage, shredded
- ½ cup diced celery
- 1 (1-pound / 454-g) can tomatoes
- ½ teaspoon salt
- ½ teaspoon dried oregano
- 1 tablespoon minced parsley
- ¼ cup each frozen corn, peas, and lima beans
- ¼ teaspoon pepper
- Grated Parmesan or Romano cheese

1. Cook macaroni according to package directions. Set aside. 2. Combine all ingredients except macaroni and cheese in large crock pot. 3. Cover. Cook on low 8 hours. Add macaroni during last 30 minutes of cooking time. 4. Garnish individual servings with cheese.

Chicken Cassoulet Soup

Prep time: 35 minutes | Cook time: 6 hours | Serves 7

- ½ pound (227 g) bulk pork sausage
- 5 cups water
- ½ pound (227 g) cubed cooked chicken
- 1 (16-ounce / 454-g) can kidney beans, rinsed and drained
- 1 (15-ounce / 425-g) can black beans, rinsed and drained
- 1 (15-ounce / 425-g) can garbanzo beans or chickpeas, rinsed and drained
- 2 medium carrots, shredded
- 1 medium onion, chopped
- ¼ cup dry vermouth or chicken broth
- 5 teaspoons chicken bouillon granules
- 4 garlic cloves, minced
- 1 teaspoon dried lavender flowers (optional)
- ½ teaspoon dried thyme
- ¼ teaspoon fennel seed, crushed
- ½ pound (227 g) bacon strips, cooked and crumbled

1. In a large skillet, brown the sausage over medium heat until it is no longer pink, then drain the excess fat. 2. Transfer the cooked sausage to a 4- or 5-quart crock pot. Add the water, chicken, beans, carrots, onion, vermouth, bouillon, garlic, and optional lavender, along with thyme and fennel. Stir to combine, then cover the pot and cook on low for 6 to 8 hours until everything is heated through and flavors meld. 3. Once cooked, ladle the mixture into bowls and top each serving with a sprinkle of crispy bacon for added flavor.

Classic Cajun Chicken Gumbo

Prep time: 25 minutes | Cook time: 4 to 10 hours | Serves 8 to 10

- ½ cup vegetable oil
- ½ cup all-purpose flour
- 1½ cups chopped onions
- 1½ cups chopped celery
- 1½ cups chopped green bell peppers
- 4 cloves garlic, minced
- 1 tablespoon Old Bay or Creole seasoning
- 1 pound (454 g) andouille or other smoked sausage, cut into ½-inch dice
- 4 cups chicken broth
- 3 cups bite-size pieces cooked chicken
- 1 bay leaf
- 3 cups cooked long-grain rice
- 6 green onions, chopped, using the white and tender green part,, for garnish
- Gumbo filé powder for serving
- Assorted hot sauces for serving

1. Heat the oil in a large skillet over medium-high heat. Add the flour and whisk to combine. Reduce the heat to medium and whisk the roux until it is a dark golden-brown, 15 to 20 minutes. 2. Add the onions, celery, bell peppers, garlic, and seasoning and sauté until the vegetables are softened, about 5 minutes. (At this point, the mixture can be refrigerated for up to 24 hours. Rewarm the roux before adding it to the crock pot.) 3. Transfer the contents of the skillet to the insert of a 5- to 7-quart crock pot and stir in the sausage, broth, chicken, and bay leaf. Cook on high for 4 to 5 hours or on low for 8 to 10 hours. Remove the bay leaf from the gumbo. 4. Serve the gumbo over the rice and garnish with the green onions. Serve with the filé powder and assorted hot sauces on the side.

Hearty Mushroom Sirloin Stew

Prep time: 20 minutes | Cook time: 6 to 7½ hours | Serves 8 to 10

- 1 pound (454 g) sirloin, cubed
- 2 tablespoons flour
- Oil
- 1 large onion, chopped
- 2 garlic cloves, minced
- ½ pound (227 g) button mushrooms, sliced
- 2 ribs celery, sliced
- 2 carrots, sliced
- 3 to 4 large potatoes, cubed
- 2 teaspoons seasoned salt
- 1 (14½-ounce / 411-g) can beef stock, or 2 bouillon cubes dissolved in 1⅔ cups water
- ½ to 1 cup good red wine

1. Dredge sirloin in flour and brown in skillet. Reserve drippings. Place meat in crock pot. 2. Sauté onion, garlic, and mushrooms in drippings just until soft. Add to meat. 3. Add all remaining ingredients. 4. Cover. Cook on low 6 hours. Test to see if vegetables are tender. If not, continue cooking on low for another 1 to 1½ hours. 5. Serve.

Lilli's Hearty Vegetable-Beef Soup

Prep time: 25 minutes | Cook time: 8 to 10 hours | Serves 10 to 12

- 3 pounds (1.4 kg) stewing meat, cut in 1-inch pieces
- 2 tablespoons oil
- 4 potatoes, cubed
- 4 carrots, sliced
- 3 ribs celery, sliced
- 1 (14-ounce / 397-g) diced tomatoes
- 1 (14-ounce / 397-g) Italian tomatoes, crushed
- 2 medium onions, chopped
- 2 wedges cabbage, sliced thinly
- 2 beef bouillon cubes
- 2 tablespoons fresh parsley
- 1 teaspoon seasoned salt
- 1 teaspoon garlic salt
- ½ teaspoon pepper
- Water

1. Brown meat in oil in skillet. Drain. 2. Combine all ingredients except water in large crock pot. Cover with water. 3. Cover. Cook on low 8 to 10 hours.

Chicken Avgolemono

Prep time: 15 minutes | Cook time: 7 hours | Serves 2

- 2 bone-in, skinless chicken breasts
- 3⅔ cups chicken stock
- 1 onion, chopped
- 2 garlic cloves, minced
- 1 carrot, chopped
- ⅓ cup basmati rice
- ½ teaspoon salt
- ½ cup heavy cream
- ¼ cup sour cream
- 3 tablespoons freshly squeezed lemon juice
- 1 tablespoon cornstarch

1. In the crock pot, combine the chicken, stock, diced onion, minced garlic, carrot, rice, and salt. Stir everything together until well mixed. 2. Cover the pot and set it to cook on low for 6½ hours, allowing the flavors to blend. 3. Once cooking is complete, carefully remove the chicken from the soup. Discard the bones or save them for making stock, and shred the chicken meat before returning it to the soup. 4. In a medium bowl, whisk together the cream, sour cream, lemon juice, and cornstarch. Gradually add 1 cup of hot liquid from the soup to the mixture and whisk until smooth. 5. Stir the cream mixture back into the soup and cook on high for an additional 15 minutes, or until the soup has thickened slightly. 6. Serve the soup hot by ladling it into two bowls. Enjoy!

Chet's Hearty Trucker Stew

Prep time: 15 minutes | Cook time: 2 to 3 hours | Serves 8

- 1 pound (454 g) bulk pork sausage, cooked and drained
- 1 pound (454 g) ground beef, cooked and drained
- 1 (31-ounce / 879-g) can pork and beans
- 1 (16-ounce / 454-g) can light kidney beans
- 1 (16-ounce / 454-g) can

- dark kidney beans
- 1 (14½-ounce / 411-g) can waxed beans, drained
- 1 (14½-ounce / 411-g) can lima beans, drained
- 1 cup ketchup
- 1 cup brown sugar
- 1 tablespoon spicy prepared mustard

1. Combine all ingredients in crock pot. 2. Cover. Simmer on high 2 to 3 hours.

Hearty Pinto Bean & Ham Soup

Prep time: 10 minutes | Cook time: 10 hours | Serves 10

- 1 pound (454 g) dried pinto beans
- 5½ cups water
- ¼ pound (113 g) cooked ham, chopped
- 1 clove garlic, minced

- 1 tablespoon chili powder
- 1 teaspoon salt
- 1 teaspoon black pepper
- ¼ teaspoon dried oregano
- ¼ teaspoon ground cumin

1. Cover bean with water and soak overnight, or 6 to 8 hours. 2. In the morning, drain and rinse beans, discard soaking water, and put beans in crock pot. 3. Add remaining ingredients, including 5½ cups fresh water. 4. Cover. Cook on low 10 hours. 5. Stir once or twice if possible during cooking time.

Nancy's Vegetable Beef Soup

Prep time: 10 minutes | Cook time: 8 hours | Serves 6 to 8

- 1 (2-pound / 907-g) roast cut into bite-sized pieces, or 2 pounds (907 g) stewing meat
- 1 (15-ounce / 425-g) can corn
- 1 (15-ounce / 425-g) can green beans
- 1 (1-pound / 454-g) bag

- frozen peas
- 1 (40-ounce / 1.1-kg) can stewed tomatoes
- 5 beef bouillon cubes
- Tabasco to taste
- 2 teaspoons salt

1. In the crock pot, combine all the ingredients, making sure not to drain the vegetables. 2. Pour in enough water to fill the crock pot to within 3 inches of the top. 3. Cover the pot and cook on low for 8 hours, or until the meat is tender and the vegetables are soft.

Savory White Bean & Barley Soup

Prep time: 15 minutes | Cook time: 8 to 10 hours | Serves 12

- 1 large onion, chopped
- 2 garlic cloves, minced
- 1 tablespoon olive or canola oil
- 2 (24-ounce / 680-g) cans Great Northern beans, undrained
- 4 cups no-fat, low-sodium chicken broth
- 4 cups water
- 2 large carrots, chunked

- 2 medium green or red bell peppers, chunked
- 2 celery ribs, chunked
- ½ cup quick-cooking barley
- ¼ cup chopped fresh parsley
- 2 bay leaves
- ½ teaspoon dried thyme
- ¼ teaspoon black pepper
- 1 (28-ounce / 794-g) can diced tomatoes, undrained

1. Sauté onion and garlic in oil in skillet until just wilted. 2. Combine all ingredients in crock pot. 3. Cook on low 8 to 10 hours. 4. Discard bay leaves before serving.

Spicy Sausage Soup

Prep time: 25 minutes | Cook time: 6 to 8 hours | Serves 8 to 10

- 1 pound (454 g) ground beef
- 1 pound (454 g) bulk spicy sausage (casings removed)
- Half a large onion, chopped
- 2 cups chopped carrots
- 2 cups chopped celery
- 1 green or red bell pepper, chopped (optional)
- 2 teaspoons salt, or to taste
- ¼ teaspoon pepper, or to

- taste
- 1 teaspoon dried oregano, or to taste
- 2 or 3 garlic cloves, minced
- 1 (14½-ounce / 411-g) can stewed tomatoes with chilies
- 1 (14½-ounce / 411-g) can green beans
- ¼ teaspoon chili powder
- 1 cup instant rice, uncooked

1. In a mixing bowl, combine the beef, sausage, and onions, then form the mixture into meatballs. Place the meatballs in the crock pot. 2. Add all the remaining ingredients to the crock pot, except for the rice. Stir gently to combine, being careful not to break apart the meatballs. 3. Cover the crock pot and cook on low for 6 to 8 hours. Stir in the rice about 20 minutes before serving. 4. Once cooked, serve hot and enjoy!

Savory Beef Barley Soup

Prep time: 15 minutes | Cook time: 9¼ to 11½ hours | Serves 8 to 10

- 3 to 4 pounds (1.4 to 1.8 kg) chuck roast
- 2 cups carrots, chopped
- 6 cups vegetable or tomato juice, divided
- 2 cups quick-cook barley
- Water, to desired consistency
- Salt and pepper to taste (optional)

1. Place roast, carrots, and 4 cups juice in crock pot. 2. Cover and cook on low 8 to 10 hours. 3. Remove roast. Place on platter and cover with foil to keep warm. 4. Meanwhile, add barley to crock pot. Stir well. Turn heat to high and cook 45 minutes to 1 hour, until barley is tender. 5. While barley is cooking, cut meat into bite-sized pieces. 6. When barley is tender, return chopped beef to crock pot. Add 2 cups juice, water if you wish, and salt and pepper, if you want. Cook for 30 minutes on high, or until soup is heated through.

Velvety Butternut Squash Soup

Prep time: 5 minutes | Cook time: 4 to 8 hours | Serves 4 to 6

- 1 (45-ounce / 1.3-kg) can chicken broth
- 1 medium butternut squash, peeled and cubed
- 1 small onion, chopped
- 1 teaspoon ground ginger
- 1 teaspoon garlic, minced (optional)
- ¼ teaspoon nutmeg (optional)

1. Place chicken broth and squash in crock pot. Add remaining ingredients. 2. Cover and cook on high 4 hours, or on low 6 to 8 hours, or until squash is tender.

Toscano Soup

Prep time: 20 minutes | Cook time: 6 to 8 hours | Serves 4 to 6

- 2 medium russet potatoes
- 1 pound (454 g) spicy Italian sausage
- 5½ cups chicken stock or low-sodium chicken broth
- 2 cups chopped kale
- ½ teaspoon crushed red pepper flakes (optional)
- ½ cup cream or evaporated milk

1. Begin by cutting the potatoes into ½-inch cubes and placing them in the crock pot. 2. Cook the sausage by grilling, broiling, or browning it in a nonstick skillet. Once it's cool enough to handle,

slice the sausage into ½-inch-thick pieces. 3. Add the sliced sausage to the crock pot, then stir in all the remaining ingredients, reserving the cream for later. 4. Cover the crock pot and cook on low for 6 to 8 hours, allowing the flavors to meld. 5. About 15 to 20 minutes before serving, stir in the cream or evaporated milk and continue to cook until the soup is heated through. Enjoy your hearty soup!

Slow-Cooked Garden Tomato Soup

Prep time: 15 minutes | Cook time: 7 hours | Serves 2

- 1 (28 ounces / 794 g) can whole tomatoes, undrained
- 1 onion, chopped
- ½ cup shredded carrot
- ½ cup chopped celery stalk
- 3 garlic cloves, minced
- 2 cups vegetable broth
- 1 teaspoon dried basil leaves
- ½ teaspoon salt
- ⅛ teaspoon freshly ground black pepper
- 1 tablespoon minced fresh thyme leaves

1. In the crock pot, combine all the ingredients except the fresh thyme leaves. 2. Cover and cook on low for 7 hours. 3. Purée the soup using an immersion blender, or purée in small batches in a food processor or blender. 4. Ladle the soup into 2 bowls, garnish with the fresh thyme leaves, and serve.

Chicken Stew with Gnocchi

Prep time: 15 minutes | Cook time: 8 hours | Serves 2

- 4 boneless, skinless chicken thighs, cubed
- 1 leek, white part only, chopped
- 2 garlic cloves, minced
- 1 sweet potato, peeled and chopped
- ½ cup chopped tomato
- ½ teaspoon salt
- ½ teaspoon dried basil leaves
- ⅛ teaspoon freshly ground black pepper
- 3 cups chicken stock
- 1 cup potato gnocchi

1. In the crock pot, mix together all the ingredients except for the gnocchi. 2. Cover the pot and set it to cook on low for 7½ hours, allowing the flavors to develop. 3. After the initial cooking time, add the gnocchi to the mixture. Cover the pot again and switch the setting to high, cooking for an additional 25 to 30 minutes, or until the gnocchi are tender. 4. Once cooked, ladle the stew into two bowls and serve hot.

Southern Italian Chicken Stew

Prep time: 15 minutes | Cook time: 4 hours | Serves 4

- 2 teaspoons olive oil
- 4 skinless chicken breasts, cut into 1-inch pieces
- 1 teaspoon garlic powder
- ¼ teaspoon black pepper
- ½ teaspoon sea salt
- 2 teaspoons dried oregano
- 1 (28-ounce / 794-g) can diced tomatoes with the juice
- 1 yellow onion, diced
- 2 cloves garlic, minced
- 1 (8-ounce / 227-g) package pasta
- 1 (14-ounce / 397-g) can artichoke hearts, drained and quartered
- 1 (6-ounce / 170-g) can black olives, drained

1. In a large skillet, heat the olive oil over medium-high heat until shimmering. 2. Season the chicken pieces with garlic powder, black pepper, sea salt, and oregano, ensuring they are evenly coated. 3. Sauté the chicken for 6 to 8 minutes, turning frequently until browned on all sides. Once cooked, transfer the chicken to a paper towel-lined plate to drain excess oil. 4. Place the drained chicken in the crock pot and layer it with the tomatoes, onion, and minced garlic. Cover the pot and cook on low for 4 hours. 5. About 3 hours into the cooking time, add the pasta to the crock pot, cover, and continue cooking until the pasta is tender. 6. When the cooking time is up, stir in the artichoke hearts and olives. Increase the heat to high, cover, and cook for an additional 10 minutes, or until the artichokes and olives are warmed through. Serve the dish hot.

Fruity Vegetable Beef Stew

Prep time: 25 minutes | Cook time: 5½ to 6½ hours | Serves 4

- ¾ pound (340 g) lean beef stewing meat, cut into ½-inch cubes
- 2 teaspoons canola oil
- 1 (14½-ounce / 411-g) can fat-free beef broth
- 1 (14½-ounce / 411-g) can stewed tomatoes, cut up
- 1½ cups peeled and cubed butternut squash
- 1 cup thawed, frozen corn
- 6 dried apricot or peach halves, quartered
- ½ cup chopped carrots
- 1 teaspoon dried oregano
- ¼ teaspoon salt
- ¼ teaspoon black pepper
- 2 tablespoons cornstarch
- ¼ cup water
- 2 tablespoons minced fresh parsley

1. In a nonstick skillet over medium heat, brown the meat in oil until fully cooked. 2. Transfer the browned meat to the crock pot and add the broth, tomatoes, squash, corn, apricots, carrots, oregano, salt, and pepper. Stir to combine all the ingredients. 3. Cover the crock pot and cook on high for 5 to 6 hours, or until the vegetables and meat are tender. 4. In a small bowl, mix the cornstarch with water until smooth, then stir this mixture into the stew. 5. Continue cooking on high for an additional 30 minutes, or until the stew has thickened to your liking. 6. Just before serving, stir in the fresh parsley for added flavor and garnish.

Corn and Potato Chowder

Prep time: 15 minutes | Cook time: 6 hours | Serves 2

- 2 cups frozen corn kernels, thawed, divided
- ½ cup diced onion
- 1 garlic clove, minced
- 3 Yukon Gold potatoes, peeled and diced
- 2 cups low-sodium chicken
- broth
- 1 thyme sprig
- ⅛ teaspoon sea salt
- 2 tablespoons heavy cream (optional)
- 1 scallion, white and green parts, sliced thin, for garnish

1. In the crock pot, combine 1½ cups of corn kernels, onion, garlic, potatoes, broth, thyme, and salt. Stir the mixture well, then cover the pot and cook on low for 6 hours. 2. After cooking, remove the thyme sprig and stir in the heavy cream (if using). Use an immersion blender to purée the soup until it reaches a smooth consistency. 3. To serve, garnish each bowl with the remaining ½ cup of corn kernels and sliced scallions for a fresh touch.

Hearty Vegetable Salmon Chowder

Prep time: 15 minutes | Cook time: 3 hours | Serves 8

- 1½ cups cubed potatoes
- 1 cup diced celery
- ½ cup diced onions
- 2 tablespoons fresh parsley, or 1 tablespoon dried parsley
- ½ teaspoon salt
- ¼ teaspoon black pepper
- Water to cover
- 1 (16-ounce / 454-g) can pink salmon
- 4 cups skim milk
- 2 teaspoons lemon juice
- 2 tablespoons finely cut red bell peppers
- 2 tablespoons finely shredded carrots
- ½ cup instant potatoes

1. Combine cubed potatoes, celery, onions, parsley, salt, pepper, and water to cover in crock pot. 2. Cook on high for 3 hours, or until soft. Add a bit more water if needed. 3. Add salmon, milk, lemon juice, red peppers, carrots, and instant potatoes. 4. Heat 1 hour more until very hot.

Garlicky Chicken Kale Soup

Prep time: 15 minutes | Cook time: 6 hours | Serves 2

- 2 boneless, skinless chicken thighs, diced
- 1 small onion, halved and sliced thin
- 2 carrots, peeled and diced
- 6 garlic cloves, roughly chopped
- 2 cups low-sodium chicken broth
- ⅛ teaspoon sea salt
- ⅛ teaspoon red pepper flakes
- Zest of 1 lemon
- Juice of 1 lemon
- 2 cups shredded fresh kale

1. In the crock pot, add the chicken, chopped onion, sliced carrots, minced garlic, broth, salt, red pepper flakes, and lemon zest. Stir the mixture well to combine all the ingredients. 2. Cover the pot and set it to cook on low for 6 hours, allowing the flavors to develop. 3. Just before serving, stir in the lemon juice and chopped kale, mixing until the kale is wilted. Serve hot and enjoy!

Hearty Sauerkraut Tomato Soup

Prep time: 10 minutes | Cook time: 4 to 6 hours | Serves 4

- 2 (14½-ounce / 411-g) cans stewed tomatoes
- 2 cups sauerkraut
- 1 cup diced potatoes
- 1 pound (454 g) fresh or smoked sausage, sliced

1. Combine all ingredients in crock pot. 2. Cover and cook on low 4 to 6 hours, or until the flavors have blended and the soup is thoroughly heated.

Mexican Black Bean Soup

Prep time: 10 minutes | Cook time: 6 to 8 hours | Serves 8

- 1 (28-ounce / 794-g) can fat-free low-sodium chicken broth
- 1 cup chopped onions
- 2 teaspoons minced garlic
- 3 cups fat-free black beans
- 2 teaspoons chili powder
- ¾ teaspoon ground cumin
- 1 (28-ounce / 794-g) can Mexican tomatoes with green chilies or jalapeños
- ¾ teaspoon lemon juice
- 1 bunch green onions
- Fat-free sour cream

1. In the crock pot, combine all the ingredients, reserving the green onions and sour cream for later. 2. Cover the pot and set it to cook on low for 6 to 8 hours, allowing the flavors to meld together. 3. When ready to serve, top each individual serving with sliced green onions and a dollop of sour cream for added flavor. Enjoy!

Ultimate Homemade Veggie Stock

Prep time: 20 minutes | Cook time: 5 to 10 hours | Makes about 8 cups

- ¼ cup olive oil
- 2 large sweet onions, such as Vidalia, coarsely chopped
- 4 large carrots, cut into 1-inch chunks
- 4 stalks celery with leaves, cut into 2-inch pieces
- 4 medium parsnips, cut into 1-inch chunks
- 8 ounces (227 g) cremini
- mushrooms, quartered
- 2 tablespoons tomato paste
- 1 bunch Swiss chard, cut into 1-inch pieces (about 3 cups)
- 2 teaspoons dried thyme
- 1 bay leaf
- 2 teaspoons salt
- ½ teaspoon whole black peppercorns
- 2 cups water

1. Put all the ingredients into the insert of a 5- to 7-quart crock pot and toss to combine. Cover and cook on high for 5 hours or on low for 8 to 10 hours. 2. Remove the cover and take out the large pieces of vegetables with a slotted spoon. Strain the stock through a fine-mesh sieve and discard the solids. 3. Skim off any fat from the top of the stock. Refrigerate for up to 5 days or freeze for up to 6 months.

Hearty Tomato-Loaded Beef Stew

Prep time: 15 minutes | Cook time: 5½ to 6 hours | Serves 6

- 2 pounds (907 g) extra-lean stewing beef cubes, trimmed of fat
- 5 to 6 carrots, cut in 1-inch pieces
- 1 large onion, cut in chunks
- 3 ribs celery, sliced
- 6 medium tomatoes, cut up and gently mashed
- ½ cup quick-cooking tapioca
- 1 whole clove, or ¼ to ½ teaspoon ground cloves
- 1 teaspoon dried basil
- ½ teaspoon dried oregano
- 2 bay leaves
- 2 teaspoons salt
- ½ teaspoon black pepper
- 3 to 4 potatoes, cubed

1. Place all ingredients in crock pot. Mix together well. 2. Cover. Cook on high 5½ to 6 hours.

Creamy Corn and Turkey Soup

Prep time: 15 minutes | Cook time: 3 to 8 hours | Serves 5 to 6

- 2 cups cooked turkey, shredded
- 1 cup milk
- 2 cups chicken broth
- 1 (15-ounce / 425-g) can

- Mexican-style corn
- 4 ounces (113 g) cream cheese, cubed
- 1 red bell pepper, chopped (optional)

1. Add all the ingredients to the crock pot, ensuring they are well distributed. 2. Cover the pot and set it to cook on low for 7 to 8 hours, or on high for 3 hours, allowing the flavors to develop.

Creamy Bacon Corn Chowder

Prep time: 15 minutes | Cook time: 6 to 7 hours | Serves 4

- 6 slices bacon, diced
- ½ cup chopped onions
- 2 cups diced peeled potatoes
- 2 (10-ounce / 283-g) packages frozen corn
- 1 (16-ounce / 454-g) can cream-style corn

- 1 tablespoon sugar
- 1 teaspoon Worcestershire sauce
- 1 teaspoon seasoned salt
- ¼ teaspoon pepper
- 1 cup water

1. In skillet, brown bacon until crisp. Remove bacon, reserving drippings. 2. Add onions and potatoes to skillet and sauté for 5 minutes. Drain. 3. Combine all ingredients in crock pot. Mix well. 4. Cover. Cook on low 6 to 7 hours.

Chinese Chicken Soup

Prep time: 5 minutes | Cook time: 1 to 2 hours | Serves 6

- 3 (14½-ounce / 411-g) cans chicken broth
- 1 (16-ounce / 454-g) package frozen stir-fry vegetable blend

- 2 cups cooked chicken, cubed
- 1 teaspoon minced fresh ginger root
- 1 teaspoon soy sauce

1. In the crock pot, mix together all the ingredients until well combined. 2. Cover the pot and cook on high for 1 to 2 hours, adjusting the time based on your preference for how crunchy or soft you like your vegetables. Enjoy your dish!

Chili-Taco Soup

Prep time: 30 minutes | Cook time: 5 to 7 hours | Serves 8

- 2 pounds (907 g) lean stew meat
- 2 (15-ounce / 425-g) cans stewed tomatoes, Mexican or regular
- 1 envelope dry taco

- seasoning mix
- 2 (15-ounce / 425-g) cans pinto beans
- 1 (15-ounce / 425-g) can whole-kernel corn
- ¾ cup water

1. Cut the larger pieces of stew meat in half and brown them in a large nonstick skillet over medium-high heat. 2. In the crock pot, combine the browned meat with all the remaining ingredients, stirring to mix well. 3. Cover the crock pot and cook on low for 5 to 7 hours, allowing the flavors to meld and the meat to become tender. Enjoy your delicious stew!

Split Pea with Chicken Soup

Prep time: 20 minutes | Cook time: 4 to 10 hours | Serves 6 to 8

- 1 (16-ounce / 454-g) package dried split peas
- ¾ cup finely diced carrots

- 3 cups cubed raw potatoes
- 8 cups chicken broth
- 1 cup cooked chicken, cubed

1. In the crock pot, combine the peas, carrots, potatoes, and chicken broth. 2. Cook on high for 4 to 5 hours or on low for 8 to 10 hours, until all the vegetables are tender. Remember to stir the soup after it starts to simmer gently. 3. About 10 minutes before serving, stir in the cooked chicken to heat through. Enjoy your hearty soup!

Easy Mix-and-Go Vegetable Soup

Prep time: 5 minutes | Cook time: 5 to 7 hours | Serves 4

- 2 cups frozen vegetables
- ¾ cup fat-free, low-sodium beef gravy
- 1 (16-ounce / 454-g) can diced tomatoes

- ¼ cup dry red wine
- ½ cup diced onions
- 1 teaspoon crushed garlic
- ¼ teaspoon black pepper
- ½ cup water

1. Combine all ingredients in crock pot. 2. Cover. Cook on high 5 hours or on low 7 hours.

Creamy Vegetable Cheese Chowder

Prep time: 15 minutes | Cook time: 4 to 10 hours | Serves 5

- 2 cups cream-style corn
- 1 cup peeled and chopped potatoes
- 1 cup peeled and chopped carrots
- 2 (14½-ounce / 411-g) cans vegetable or chicken broth
- 1 (16-ounce / 454-g) jar processed cheese

1. Combine all ingredients except cheese in the crock pot. 2. Cover and cook on low 8 to 10 hours, or on high 4 to 5 hours. 3. Thirty to 60 minutes before serving, stir in the cheese. Then cook on high for 30 to 60 minutes to melt and blend the cheese.

Hamburger Vegetable Soup

Prep time: 20 minutes | Cook time: 8 to 9 hours | Serves 8 to 10

- 1 pound (454 g) ground chuck
- 1 onion, chopped
- 2 garlic cloves, minced
- 4 cups V-8 juice
- 1 (14½-ounce / 411-g) can stewed tomatoes
- 2 cups coleslaw mix
- 2 cups frozen green beans
- 2 cups frozen corn
- 2 tablespoons Worcestershire sauce
- 1 teaspoon dried basil
- ½ teaspoon salt
- ¼ teaspoon pepper

1. In a skillet, brown the beef along with the onion and garlic until fully cooked. Drain any excess fat, then transfer the mixture to the crock pot. 2. Add the remaining ingredients to the crock pot and stir well to combine everything evenly. 3. Cover the pot and cook on low for 8 to 9 hours, allowing the flavors to meld together.

Busy Cook's Stew

Prep time: 30 minutes | Cook time: 6 to 8 hours | Serves 4 to 6

- 1 pound (454 g) boneless stew meat, cut up
- 1 (10¾-ounce / 305-g) can cream of mushroom soup
- 2 cups water
- 3 potatoes, cubed
- 3 carrots, diced
- 1 onion, chopped

1. In a large nonstick skillet, brown the meat over medium-high heat, ensuring not to overcrowd the pan so that the meat can brown evenly on all sides. If your skillet is 10 inches or smaller, brown the meat in two separate batches. 2. Transfer the browned meat to the crock pot. Then, add the remaining ingredients in the order they are listed, stirring well after each addition to combine everything thoroughly. 3. Cover the crock pot and set it to cook on low for 6 to 8 hours, or until both the meat and vegetables are tender but still hold their shape. Be sure to stir occasionally during the cooking process.

The Tabasco Veggie Soup

Prep time: 20 minutes | Cook time: 9 hours | Serves 8

- 2 (14½-ounce / 411-g) cans vegetable broth
- 2 vegetable bouillon cubes
- 4 cups water
- 1 quart canned tomatoes
- 3 to 4 garlic cloves, minced
- 1 large onion, chopped
- 1 cup chopped celery
- 2 cups chopped carrots
- 1 small zucchini, cubed
- 1 small yellow squash, cubed
- 2 teaspoons fresh basil
- 1 teaspoon fresh parsley
- Pepper to taste
- 3 dashes Tabasco sauce

1. Place all the ingredients into the crock pot and mix them together. 2. Cover the pot securely and set it to cook on low for 9 hours.

Smoky Spiced Lentil & Chickpea Stew

Prep time: 25 minutes | Cook time: 8 hours | Serves 8

- 2 teaspoons olive oil
- 1 medium onion, thinly sliced
- 1 teaspoon dried oregano
- ½ teaspoon crushed red pepper flakes
- 2 (15-ounce / 425-g) cans chickpeas or garbanzo beans, rinsed and drained
- 1 cup dried lentils, rinsed
- 1 (2¼-ounce / 64-g) can sliced ripe olives, drained
- 3 teaspoons smoked paprika
- 4 cups vegetable broth
- 4 (8-ounce / 227-g) cans no-salt-added tomato sauce
- 4 cups fresh baby spinach
- ¾ cup fat-free plain yogurt

1. In a small skillet, heat oil over medium-high heat. Add onion, oregano and pepper flakes; cook and stir 8 to 10 minutes or until onion is tender. Transfer to a 5- or 6-quart crock pot. 2. Add chickpeas, lentils, olives and paprika; stir in broth and tomato sauce. Cook, covered, on low 8 to 10 hours or until lentils are tender. Stir in spinach. Top with yogurt.

Thai-Inspired Coconut Chicken Soup

Prep time: 15 minutes | Cook time: 8 hours | Serves 2

- 5 boneless, skinless chicken thighs
- 1 cup sliced shiitake or cremini mushrooms
- 2 garlic cloves, minced
- 2 teaspoons grated fresh ginger
- ½ teaspoon lime zest
- 2 cups chicken stock
- 1 cup coconut milk
- 1 tablespoon freshly squeezed lime juice
- 1 tablespoon Thai fish sauce
- 1 teaspoon curry powder
- 1 cup fresh snap peas
- ½ red bell pepper, cut with spiral cutter, if desired
- ¼ cucumber, cut with spiral cutter, if desired

1. In the crock pot, combine all the ingredients except the snap peas, bell pepper, and cucumber. 2. Cover and cook on low for 7½ hours, or until the chicken is tender. 3. Remove the chicken from the soup and shred; return the chicken to the crock pot. 4. Add the snap peas to the crock pot, cover, and cook on low for 20 minutes more, until crisp-tender. 5. Ladle the soup into 2 bowls and serve. Garnish with the spiral-cut red bell pepper and cucumber.

Savory Curried Meatball Soup

Prep time: 40 minutes | Cook time: 4 hours | Serves 8

Meat Balls:
- 1 cup cooked long-grain rice
- 1½ pounds (680 g) 85-percent lean ground beef
- 1 teaspoon sweet curry powder
- 2 tablespoons soy sauce

Soup:
- 7 cups beef broth
- ½ cup soy sauce
- 1 bunch bok choy, cut into 1-inch pieces (about 2 cups)

- 4 green onions, finely chopped, using the white and tender green parts
- 1 tablespoon Major Grey's chutney or other mild chutney
- 1 large egg, beaten
- 1 cup snow peas, ends trimmed and strings removed
- 2 cups fresh bean sprouts or other sprouts such as radish or broccoli, for garnish

1. Put all the meatball ingredients in a large bowl and stir to combine. Using a small scoop, form the meat into 1-inch balls. 2. Add the broth and soy sauce to the insert of a 5- to 7-quart crock pot. 3. Add the meatballs, cover, and cook on high for 3 hours, until the meatballs float to the top. Skim off any foam that may have formed from the top of the broth. 4. Add the bok choy and snow peas to the cooker and cook on low for an additional 1 hour, until the bok choy is tender. 5. Serve the soup garnished with the fresh bean sprouts.

Hearty Sauerkraut & Potato Soup

Prep time: 15 minutes | Cook time: 2 to 8 hours | Serves 8

- 1 pound (454 g) smoked Polish sausage, cut into ½-inch pieces
- 5 medium potatoes, cubed
- 2 large onions, chopped
- 2 large carrots, cut into ¼-inch slices
- 1 (42-ounce / 1.2-kg) can chicken broth
- 1 (32-ounce / 907-g) can or bag sauerkraut, rinsed and drained
- 1 (6-ounce / 170-g) can tomato paste

1. Combine all ingredients in large crock pot. Stir to combine. 2. Cover. Cook on high 2 hours, and then on low 6 to 8 hours. 3. Serve.

Homemade Sausage Soup

Prep time: 15 minutes | Cook time: 6 hours | Serves 6

- 3 tablespoons olive oil, divided
- 1½ pounds (680 g) sausage, without casing
- 6 cups chicken broth
- 2 celery stalks, chopped
- 1 carrot, diced
- 1 leek, thoroughly cleaned and chopped
- 2 teaspoons minced garlic
- 2 cups chopped kale
- 1 tablespoon chopped fresh parsley, for garnish

1. Begin by lightly greasing the insert of the crock pot with 1 tablespoon of olive oil. 2. In a large skillet over medium-high heat, warm the remaining 2 tablespoons of olive oil. Add the sausage and sauté until it is fully cooked, which should take about 7 minutes. 3. Transfer the cooked sausage to the crock pot insert, then stir in the broth along with the celery, carrot, leek, and minced garlic. 4. Cover the crock pot and cook on low for 6 hours, allowing the flavors to meld. 5. About 10 minutes before serving, stir in the kale until wilted. 6. Serve the soup hot, garnished with fresh parsley for added flavor and color. Enjoy!

Mexican Tomato-Corn Soup

Prep time: 10 minutes | Cook time: 6 to 8 hours | Serves 8

- 1 medium onion, diced
- 1 medium green bell pepper, diced
- 1 clove garlic, minced
- 1 cup diced carrots
- 1 (14½-ounce / 411-g) can low-sodium diced Italian tomatoes
- 2½ cups low-sodium tomato juice
- 1 quart low-fat, low-sodium chicken broth
- 3 cups corn, frozen or canned
- 1 (4-ounce / 113-g) can chopped chilies, undrained
- 1 teaspoon chili powder
- 1½ teaspoons ground cumin
- Dash cayenne powder

1. In the crock pot, add all the ingredients and mix them together well. 2. Cover the pot and set it to cook on low for 6 to 8 hours, allowing the flavors to blend and develop. Enjoy your dish!

Hearty Lentil & Tomato Stew

Prep time: 10 minutes | Cook time: 4 to 12 hours | Serves 8

- 3 cups water
- 1 (28-ounce / 794-g) can low-sodium peeled Italian tomatoes, undrained
- 1 (6-ounce / 170-g) can low-sodium tomato paste
- ½ cup dry red wine
- ¾ teaspoon dried basil
- ¾ teaspoon dried thyme
- ½ teaspoon crushed red pepper
- 1 pound (454 g) dried lentils, rinsed and drained with any stones removed
- 1 large onion, chopped
- 4 medium carrots, cut in ½-inch rounds
- 4 medium celery ribs, cut into ½-inch slices
- 3 garlic cloves, minced
- 1 teaspoon salt
- Chopped fresh basil or parsley, for garnish

1. Combine water, tomatoes with juice, tomato paste, red wine, basil, thyme, and crushed red pepper in crock pot. 2. Break up tomatoes with a wooden spoon and stir to blend them and the paste into the mixture. 3. Add lentils, onion, carrots, celery, and garlic. 4. Cover. Cook on low 10 to 12 hours, or on high 4 to 5 hours. 5. Stir in the salt. 6. Serve in bowls, sprinkled with chopped basil or parsley.

Asian Pork Soup

Prep time: 20 minutes | Cook time: 3 to 9 hours | Serves 6

- 1 pound (454 g) lean uncooked pork or chicken, cut in ½-inch cubes
- 2 medium carrots, cut in julienne strips
- 4 medium green onions, chopped
- 1 clove garlic, finely chopped
- 3 to 4 tablespoons low-sodium soy sauce, according to your taste
- preference
- ½ teaspoon finely chopped ginger root
- ⅛ teaspoon black pepper
- 1 (10¾-ounce / 305-g) can fat-free, reduced-sodium beef broth
- 1 cup fresh mushrooms, sliced
- 1 cup bean sprouts

1. In a large nonstick skillet, cook the meat over medium heat for 8 to 10 minutes, stirring occasionally until browned. 2. In the crock pot, combine the cooked meat with all the remaining ingredients except for the mushrooms and bean sprouts. 3. Cover the crock pot and cook on low for 7 to 9 hours, or on high for 3 to 4 hours. 4. Once the cooking time is complete, stir in the mushrooms and bean sprouts. 5. Cover the pot again and cook on low for an additional hour to allow the flavors to meld. Enjoy your dish!

Split Pea Soup with Ham

Prep time: 15 minutes | Cook time: 4 hours | Serves 8

- 2½ quarts water
- 1 ham hock or pieces of cut-up ham
- 2½ cups split peas, dried
- 1 medium onion, chopped
- 3 medium carrots, cut in small pieces
- Salt and pepper to taste

1. Start by bringing water to a boil in a saucepan on the stovetop. 2. In the crock pot, combine all the other ingredients and then add the boiled water, stirring everything together thoroughly. 3. Cover the crock pot and cook on high for 4 hours, or until the vegetables are tender. 4. If you included a ham hock, carefully remove it from the soup once it's cooked, debone the meat, and stir the chopped meat back into the soup before serving. Enjoy your hearty dish!

Veracruz-Inspired Fish Soup

Prep time: 30 minutes | Cook time: 5 to 6 hours | Serves 8

- 4 (6-inch) corn tortillas, cut into thin strips
- 2 tablespoons vegetable oil
- 1 medium onion, finely chopped
- 2 cloves garlic, minced
- 1 jalapeño pepper, seeded and finely chopped
- 2 medium red bell peppers, finely chopped
- 1 teaspoon ground cumin
- 1 teaspoon dried oregano
- 1 (12-ounce / 340-g) bottle Corona or other light Mexican beer
- 1 (28- to 32-ounce / 794- to 907-g) can chopped tomatoes, with their juice
- 1 (8-ounce / 227-g) bottle clam juice
- 1 pound (454 g) sea bass, halibut, or red snapper fillets, cut into 1-inch chunks
- 2 cups cooked long-grain rice
- ½ cup finely chopped fresh cilantro
- Salt and freshly ground black pepper

1. Place the tortillas in the bottom of the insert of a 5- to 7-quart crock pot. 2. Heat the oil in a large skillet over medium-high heat. Add the onion, garlic, jalapeño, bell peppers, cumin, and oregano and sauté until the vegetables are softened, about 5 minutes. 3. Deglaze the pan with the beer, scraping up any browned bits from the bottom of the skillet. Transfer the contents of the skillet to the slow-cooker insert and stir to combine with the tortillas. Stir in the tomatoes and clam juice. 4. Cover and cook on low for 4 to 5 hours. Stir in the fish, rice, and cilantro and cook for an additional 1 hour, until the fish is cooked through. 5. Season with salt and pepper before serving.

Chapter **7**

Snacks and Appetizers

Chapter 7 Snacks and Appetizers

Cider Cheese Fondue—for a Buffet Table

Prep time: 15 minutes | Cook time: 4 minutes | Serves 4

- ¾ cup apple juice or cider
- 2 cups shredded Cheddar cheese
- 1 cup shredded Swiss cheese
- 1 tablespoon cornstarch
- ⅛ teaspoon pepper
- 1 pound (454 g) loaf French bread, cut into chunks

1. In a large saucepan, bring the cider to a boil over medium-high heat. Once boiling, reduce the heat to medium-low. 2. In a large mixing bowl, combine the cheeses with cornstarch and pepper, tossing to coat evenly. 3. Gradually stir the cheese mixture into the simmering cider, cooking and stirring for 3 to 4 minutes, or until the cheese is fully melted and smooth. 4. Transfer the melted cheese mixture to a 1-quart crock pot to keep it warm, stirring occasionally. 5. Serve the warm cheese dip with bread cubes for dipping. Enjoy!

Slow-Roasted Tomato & Mozzarella Bruschetta

Prep time: 15 minutes | Cook time: 5 hours | Serves 8

- ¼ cup extra-virgin olive oil
- 1 large red onion, coarsely chopped
- 2 teaspoons dried basil
- 1 teaspoon fresh rosemary leaves, finely chopped
- 4 cloves garlic, minced
- 3 (28- to 32-ounce / 794- to 907-g) cans whole plum tomatoes, drained
- 2 teaspoons salt
- ⅛ teaspoon red pepper flakes
- 8 ounces (227 g) fresh Mozzarella, cut into ½-inch dice

1. Lightly toasted baguette slices for serving 2. Combine all the ingredients except the Mozzarella and the baguette slices in the insert of a 5- to 7-quart crock pot. Cover and cook on high for 2 hours. Uncover the cooker and cook on low, stirring occasionally, for 3 hours, until the tomato liquid has almost evaporated. 3. Remove the tomato mixture to the bowl of a food processor and pulse on and off five times to chop the tomatoes and garlic. Transfer to a serving bowl to cool, then stir in the Mozzarella. 4. Serve with the toasted baguette slices.

Savory Warm Clam Dip

Prep time: 15 minutes | Cook time: 2 to 3 hours | Serves 6 to 8

- 2 (8-ounce / 227-g) packages cream cheese at room temperature and cut into cubes
- ½ cup mayonnaise
- 3 green onions, finely chopped, using the white and tender green parts
- 2 cloves garlic, minced
- 3 (8-ounce / 227-g) cans minced or chopped clams, drained with ¼ cup clam juice reserved
- 1 tablespoon Worcestershire sauce
- 2 teaspoons anchovy paste
- ¼ cup finely chopped fresh Italian parsley

1. Coat the insert of a 1½- to 3-quart crock pot with nonstick cooking spray. Combine all the ingredients in a large mixing bowl, adding the clam juice to thin the dip. 2. Transfer the mixture to the crock pot, cover, and cook on low for 2 to 3 hours, until bubbling. 3. Serve from the cooker set on warm.

Curried Almonds

Prep time: 5 minutes | Cook time: 3 to 4½ hours | Makes 4 cups nuts

- 2 tablespoons butter, melted
- 1 tablespoon curry powder
- ½ teaspoon seasoned salt
- 1 pound (454 g) blanched almonds

1. In a small bowl, mix the butter with curry powder and seasoned salt until well combined. 2. Pour this mixture over the almonds in the crock pot, ensuring the almonds are evenly coated. 3. Cover the crock pot and cook on low for 2 to 3 hours. Then, turn the setting to high, uncover the cooker, and continue cooking for an additional 1 to 1½ hours. 4. Once done, serve the almonds hot or cold, as desired. Enjoy!

Ultimate Party Snack Mix

Prep time: 20 minutes | Cook time: 2 hours | Serves 8 to 10

½ cup (2 sticks) unsalted butter, melted	2 cups mixed nuts
2 tablespoons Lawry's seasoned salt	1 (8- to 10-ounce / 227- to 283-g) bag pretzel sticks
1 tablespoon garlic salt	1 (5-ounce / 142-g) bag plain or Parmesan goldfish crackers
¼ cup Worcestershire sauce	
6 shakes Tabasco sauce	2 (3-ounce / 85-g) bags herbed croutons
4 cups Crispix cereal	

1. Combine the butter, seasoned salt, garlic salt, Worcestershire, and Tabasco in the insert of a 5- to 7-quart crock pot and stir to blend. Add the remaining ingredients and gently stir to coat each piece with the flavored butter. 2. Cook uncovered on high for 2 hours, stirring occasionally. Reduce the heat to low and cook for an additional hour, stirring every 15 minutes, until the mix is dry and crisp. 3. Transfer to baking sheets to cool completely before serving, or store in airtight containers.

Slow Cooked Smokies

Prep time: 5 minutes | Cook time: 6 to 7 hours | Serves 12 to 16

2 pounds (907 g) miniature smoked sausage links	3 tablespoons Worcestershire sauce
1 (28-ounce / 794-g) bottle barbecue sauce	3 tablespoons steak sauce
1¼ cups water	½ teaspoon pepper

1. In the crock pot, combine all the ingredients and mix them thoroughly until well combined. 2. Cover the pot and set it to cook on low for 6 to 7 hours, allowing the flavors to meld and develop. Enjoy your dish!

Sweet & Tangy BBQ Meatballs

Prep time: 15 minutes | Cook time: 2 to 4 hours | Makes 50 to 60 meatballs

2 pounds (907 g) precooked meatballs	barbecue sauce
1 (16-ounce / 454-g) bottle	8 ounces (227 g) grape jelly

1. Place meatballs in crock pot. 2. Combine barbecue sauce and jelly in medium-sized mixing bowl. 3. Pour over meatballs and stir well. 4. Cover and cook on high 2 hours, or on low 4 hours. 5. Turn to low and serve.

Spicy Buffalo Wing Dip

Prep time: 20 minutes | Cook time: 2 hours | Makes 6 cups

2 (8-ounce / 227-g) packages cream cheese, softened	chicken
	½ cup Buffalo wing sauce
½ cup ranch salad dressing	2 cups shredded cheddar cheese, divided
½ cup sour cream	
5 tablespoons crumbled blue cheese	1 green onion, sliced
	Tortilla chips
2 cups shredded cooked	

1. In a small bowl, combine the cream cheese, dressing, sour cream and blue cheese. Transfer to a 3-quart crock pot. Layer with chicken, wing sauce and 1 cup cheese. Cover and cook on low for 2 to 3 hours or until heated through. 2. Sprinkle with remaining cheese and onion. Serve with tortilla chips.

Hot Bloody Mary Dip for Shrimp

Prep time: 15 minutes | Cook time: 3 to 4 hours | Serves 8

2 (8-ounce / 227-g) packages cream cheese at room temperature, cut into cubes	2 teaspoons celery salt
	¼ teaspoon freshly ground black pepper
1½ cups Clamato juice	
2 cups spicy tomato juice or bloody Mary mix	2 tablespoons fresh lemon juice
	1 cup pepper vodka
2 tablespoons prepared horseradish	4 green onions, finely chopped, using the white and tender green parts
⅓ cup Worcestershire sauce	
1 teaspoon Tabasco sauce	4 stalks celery, finely chopped

1. Start by coating the insert of a 3- to 5-quart crock pot with nonstick cooking spray. Place the cream cheese in the insert, cover it, and cook on low for 20 minutes, or until the cream cheese begins to melt. 2. After the initial melting, add the remaining ingredients to the crock pot and stir until well combined. 3. Cover the pot again and continue to cook on low for 3 to 4 hours, stirring occasionally during the cooking process. 4. When ready to serve, keep the cooker set on warm and enjoy your dish straight from the pot.

Savory Curry Snack Mix

Prep time: 10 minutes | Cook time: 2½ hours | Makes about 2½ quarts

- 4½ cups crispy chow mein noodles
- 4 cups Rice Chex
- 1 (9¾-ounce / 276-g) can salted cashews
- 1 cup flaked coconut, toasted
- ½ cup butter, melted
- 2 tablespoons reduced-sodium soy sauce
- 2¼ teaspoons curry powder
- ¾ teaspoon ground ginger

1. In a 5-quart crock pot, combine the noodles, cereal, cashews and coconut. In a small bowl, whisk the butter, soy sauce, curry powder and ginger; drizzle over cereal mixture and mix well. 2. Cover and cook on low for 2½ hours, stirring every 30 minutes. Serve warm or at room temperature.

Meaty Buffet Favorites

Prep time: 5 minutes | Cook time: 2 hours | Serves 24

- 1 cup tomato sauce
- 1 teaspoon Worcestershire sauce
- ½ teaspoon prepared mustard
- 2 tablespoons brown sugar
- 1 pound (454 g) prepared meatballs or mini-wieners

1. In the crock pot, combine the first four ingredients and mix well. 2. Add the meatballs or mini-wieners to the mixture, ensuring they are evenly distributed. 3. Cover the pot and cook on high for 2 hours. After that, turn the heat down to low and keep warm. 4. Serve directly from the crock pot as a delicious appetizer. Enjoy!

Orange Chipotle Wings

Prep time: 15 minutes | Cook time: 3 hours | Serves 8

- 3 pounds (1.4 kg) chicken wing drumettes
- 1 medium red onion, finely chopped
- 6 chipotle chiles in adobo, finely chopped
- 1 teaspoon ground cumin
- 2 cloves garlic, minced
- 1½ cups orange juice
- ½ cup honey
- ½ cup ketchup
- ½ cup finely chopped fresh cilantro

1. Begin by coating the insert of a 5- to 7-quart crock pot with nonstick cooking spray to prevent sticking. 2. Arrange the wings on a rack placed over a baking sheet and broil them until they are crispy on one side, about 5 to 7 minutes. 3. Flip the wings over and broil the other side until they are crispy and browned, which should take another 5 minutes. 4. Once done, remove the wings from the oven. If you prefer, you can cool the wings and refrigerate them for up to 2 days; otherwise, place the wings directly into the prepared crock pot insert. 5. In a mixing bowl, combine the remaining ingredients and pour the mixture over the wings. Toss the wings gently to ensure they are well coated with the sauce. 6. Cover the crock pot and cook the wings on high for 3 hours, turning them twice during the cooking process to promote even cooking. 7. When ready to serve, keep the wings warm in the cooker and serve directly from the pot. Enjoy!

Hearty Beef Dip Fondue

Prep time: 20 minutes | Cook time: 6 hours | Makes 2½ cups

- 1¾ cups milk
- 2 (8-ounce / 227-g) packages cream cheese, cubed
- 2 teaspoons dry mustard
- ¼ cup chopped green onions
- 2½ ounces (71 g) sliced dried beef, shredded or torn into small pieces
- French bread, cut into bite-sized pieces, each having a side of crust

1. Begin by heating the milk in the crock pot on high until it's warmed through. 2. Add the cheese to the warm milk, stirring until it has completely melted and is smooth. 3. Incorporate the mustard, green onions, and dried beef into the mixture, stirring well to combine all ingredients. 4. Cover the crock pot and reduce the heat to low, cooking for up to 6 hours to allow the flavors to meld. 5. When ready to serve, provide long forks for dipping pieces of bread into the warm cheese mixture. Enjoy!

Zesty Garlic Swiss Fondue

Prep time: 10 minutes | Cook time: 2 hours | Makes 3 cups

- 4 cups shredded Swiss cheese
- 1 (10¾-ounce / 305-g) can condensed cheddar cheese soup, undiluted
- 2 tablespoons sherry or chicken broth
- 1 tablespoon Dijon mustard
- 2 garlic cloves, minced
- 2 teaspoons hot pepper sauce
- Cubed French bread baguette
- Sliced apples
- Seedless red grapes

1. In a 1½-quart crock pot, mix the first six ingredients. Cook, covered, on low 2 to 2½ hours or until the cheese is melted, stirring every 30 minutes. Serve warm with bread cubes and fruit.

Sweet & Spicy BBQ Little Smokies

Prep time: 15 minutes | Cook time: 2 to 3 hours | Serves 6 to 8

- 2 (16-ounce / 454-g) packages mini smoked sausages (Hillshire Farms is a reliable brand)
- 2 tablespoons canola or vegetable oil
- 1 medium onion, finely chopped
- 2 teaspoons ancho chile
- powder
- 1½ cups ketchup
- 1 (8-ounce / 227-g) can tomato sauce
- ¼ cup molasses
- 2 tablespoons Worcestershire sauce
- ¼ cup honey

1. Arrange the sausages in the insert of a 1½- to 3-quart crock pot. Heat the oil in a small skillet over medium-high heat. Add the onion and chili powder and sauté until the onion is softened, about 3 minutes. 2. Transfer the contents of the skillet to the slow-cooker insert. Add the ketchup, tomato sauce, molasses, Worcestershire, and honey and stir to blend. Cover and cook over low heat 2 to 3 hours, until the sausages are heated through. 3. Serve the sausages from the cooker set on warm.

Hot Broccoli Dip

Prep time: 20 minutes | Cook time: 1 hour | Serves 24

- 2 cups fresh or frozen broccoli, chopped
- 4 tablespoons chopped red bell pepper
- 2 (8-ounce / 227-g)
- containers ranch dip
- ½ cup grated Parmesan cheese
- 2 cups shredded Cheddar cheese

1. In the crock pot, combine all the ingredients thoroughly. 2. Set the crock pot to cook on low for 1 hour. 3. Once the cooking time is complete, serve hot and enjoy!

Sweet & Tangy Party Dogs

Prep time: 15 minutes | Cook time: 1 to 2 hours | Serves 12

- 12 hot dogs, cut into bite-size pieces
- 1 cup grape jelly
- 1 cup prepared mustard

1. Place all ingredients in crock pot. Stir well. 2. Turn on high until mixture boils. Stir. 3. Turn to low and bring to the buffet table.

Slim Dunk

Prep time: 10 minutes | Cook time: 1 hour | Serves 12

- 2 cups fat-free sour cream
- ¼ cup fat-free miracle whip salad dressing
- 1 (10-ounce / 283-g) package frozen chopped spinach,
- squeezed dry and chopped
- 1 (1.8-ounce / 51-g) envelope dry leek soup mix
- ¼ cup red bell pepper, minced

1. In the crock pot, combine all the ingredients and mix them thoroughly until well combined. 2. Cover the pot and set it to cook on high for 1 hour. 3. Once the cooking time is complete, serve the dish hot and enjoy!

Herbed Pizza Party Dip

Prep time: 15 minutes | Cook time: 3 to 4 hours | Serves 8

- 2 tablespoons extra-virgin olive oil
- 1 medium onion, finely chopped
- 2 teaspoons dried oregano
- 2 teaspoons dried basil
- Pinch of red pepper flakes
- 3 cloves garlic, minced
- 2 (14- to 15-ounce / 397- to 425-g) cans crushed plum tomatoes, with their juice
- 2 tablespoons tomato paste
- 1 ½ teaspoons salt
- ½ teaspoon freshly ground black pepper
- ½ cup finely chopped fresh Italian parsley

1. Heat the oil in a small saucepan over medium-high heat. Add the onion, oregano, basil, red pepper flakes, and garlic and sauté until the onion is softened, about 3 minutes. 2. Transfer the contents of the skillet to the insert of a 1½- to 3-quart crock pot. Add the remaining ingredients and stir to combine. Cover and cook on low for 3 to 4 hours. 3. Serve from the cooker set on warm.

Barbecued Lil' Smokies

Prep time: 5 minutes | Cook time: 4 hours | Serves 48 to 60 as an appetizer

- 4 (16-ounce / 454-g) packages little smokies
- 1 (18-ounce / 510-g) bottle barbecue sauce

1. In the crock pot, mix all the ingredients together until well combined. 2. Cover the pot and cook on low for 4 hours, allowing the flavors to meld. Enjoy your dish!

Cheesy Loaded Veggie Dip

Prep time: 1 hour | Cook time: 1 hour | Makes 5 cups

- ¾ cup finely chopped fresh broccoli
- ½ cup finely chopped cauliflower
- ½ cup finely chopped fresh carrot
- ½ cup finely chopped red onion
- ½ cup finely chopped celery
- 2 garlic cloves, minced
- 4 tablespoons olive oil, divided
- 1 (14-ounce / 397-g) can water-packed artichoke hearts, rinsed, drained and chopped
- 1 (6½-ounce / 184-g)

- package spreadable garlic and herb cream cheese
- 1 (1.4-ounce / 40-g) package vegetable recipe mix (Knorr)
- 1 teaspoon garlic powder
- ½ teaspoon white pepper
- ⅛ to ¼ teaspoon cayenne pepper
- ¼ cup vegetable broth
- ¼ cup half-and-half cream
- 3 cups shredded Italian cheese blend
- ½ cup minced fresh basil
- 1 (9-ounce / 255-g) package fresh spinach, finely chopped
- Assorted crackers or baked pita chips

1. In a large skillet, saute the broccoli, cauliflower, carrot, onion, celery and garlic in 2 tablespoons oil until tender. Stir in the artichokes, cream cheese, vegetable recipe mix, garlic powder, white pepper and cayenne; set aside. 2. In a 3-quart crock pot, combine broth, cream and remaining oil. Stir in broccoli mixture, Italian cheese blend and basil. Fold in spinach. Cover and cook on low for 1 to 2 hours or until cheese is melted and spinach is tender. Serve with crackers.

Spicy Crocked Nuts

Prep time: 15 minutes | Cook time: 2 to 2½ hours | Serves 8

- 4 tablespoons (½ stick) unsalted butter, melted
- 2 teaspoons Lawry's seasoned salt
- 1 teaspoon garlic salt

- ⅛ teaspoon cayenne pepper
- 4 tablespoons sugar
- 4 cups pecan halves, walnut halves, or whole almonds

1. In the insert of a 5- to 7-quart crock pot, combine the butter, seasoned salt, garlic salt, cayenne pepper, and 2 tablespoons of sugar. Cover the pot and cook on high for 20 minutes until the butter is melted. 2. Add the nuts to the crock pot and stir to coat

them thoroughly with the butter mixture. Cook uncovered for 2 to 2½ hours, stirring occasionally to ensure even cooking. 3. After the cooking time, sprinkle the remaining 2 tablespoons of sugar over the nuts, tossing to coat evenly. Transfer the nuts to a baking sheet and allow them to cool completely before serving. Enjoy your tasty treat!

Slow-Cooked Cranberry Chutney Brie

Prep time: 10 minutes | Cook time: 4 hours | Serves 8 to 10

- 1 cup fresh or dried cranberries
- ½ cup brown sugar
- ⅓ cup cider vinegar
- 2 tablespoons water or orange juice
- 2 teaspoons minced crystallized ginger

- ¼ teaspoon cinnamon
- ⅛ teaspoon ground cloves
- Oil
- 1 (8-ounce / 227-g) round of Brie cheese
- 1 tablespoon sliced almonds, toasted
- Crackers

1. Mix together cranberries, brown sugar, vinegar, water or juice, ginger, cinnamon, and cloves in crock pot. 2. Cover. Cook on low 4 hours. Stir once near the end to see if it is thickening. If not, remove lid, turn heat to high and cook 30 minutes without lid. 3. Put cranberry chutney in covered container and chill for up to 2 weeks. When ready to serve, bring to room temperature. 4. Brush ovenproof plate with oil, place unpeeled Brie on plate, and bake uncovered at 350ºF (180ºC) for 9 minutes, until cheese is soft and partially melted. Remove from oven. 5. Top with at least half the chutney and garnish with almonds. Serve with crackers.

Warm Swiss & Dill Cheese Dip

Prep time: 10 minutes | Cook time: 2 to 3 hours | Serves 8

- 2 medium sweet onions, such as Vidalia, finely chopped
- 2 tablespoons finely chopped fresh dill
- 1½ cups mayonnaise

- 2 cups finely shredded Havarti with dill
- 2 cups finely shredded Swiss cheese

1. Coat the insert of a 1½- to 3-quart crock pot with nonstick cooking spray. Combine all the ingredients in a bowl and transfer to the crock pot. Cover and cook on low for 2 to 3 hours, until bubbling. 2. Serve from the cooker set on warm.

Sausages in Wine

Prep time: 15 minutes | Cook time: 1 hour | Serves 6

- 1 cup dry red wine
- 2 tablespoons currant jelly
- 6 to 8 mild Italian sausages or Polish sausages

1. In the crock pot, combine the wine and jelly. Heat the mixture until the jelly has dissolved and the sauce begins to simmer. Once simmering, add the sausages to the pot. 2. Cover the crock pot and cook on high for 45 minutes to 1 hour, or until the sausages are fully cooked through and lightly glazed. 3. After cooking, transfer the sausages to a cutting board and slice them into pieces. Serve hot and enjoy!

Melty Cheesy Tomato Pizza Fondue

Prep time: 15 minutes | Cook time: 1 hour | Serves 4 to 6

- 1 (1-pound / 454-g) block of cheese, your choice of good melting cheese, cut in ½-inch cubes
- 2 cups shredded Mozzarella cheese
- 1 (19-ounce / 539-g) can Italian-style stewed tomatoes with juice
- Loaf of Italian bread, slices toasted and then cut into 1-inch cubes

1. Place cheese cubes, shredded Mozzarella cheese, and tomatoes in a lightly greased crock pot. 2. Cover and cook on high 45 to 60 minutes, or until cheese is melted. 3. Stir occasionally and scrape down sides of crock pot with rubber spatula to prevent scorching. 4. Reduce heat to low and serve. (Fondue will keep a smooth consistency for up to 4 hours.) 5. Serve with toasted bread cubes for dipping.

Party Time Artichokes

Prep time: 10 minutes | Cook time: 2½ to 4 hours | Serves 4

- 4 whole, fresh artichokes
- 1 teaspoon salt
- 4 tablespoons lemon juice, divided
- 2 tablespoons butter, melted

1. Begin by washing the artichokes and trimming off the tough outer leaves and the bottom ends. Cut off about 1 inch from the tops of each artichoke and trim the tips of the leaves. Gently spread the top leaves apart and use a long-handled spoon to remove the fuzzy chokes from the centers. 2. Place the prepared artichokes upright in the crock pot and sprinkle each one with ¼ teaspoon of salt. 3. Drizzle 2 tablespoons of lemon juice over the artichokes, then pour in enough water to cover the bottom half of the artichokes. 4. Cover the crock pot and cook on high for 2½ to 4 hours, or until the artichokes are tender. 5. Serve the artichokes with melted butter and the remaining lemon juice on the side for dipping. Enjoy!

Crock Pot Candy

Prep time: 10 minutes | Cook time: 2 hours | Makes 80 to 100 pieces

- 1½ pounds (680 g) almond bark, broken
- 1 (4-ounce / 113-g) Baker's Brand German sweet chocolate bar, broken

- 8 ounces (227 g) chocolate chips
- 8 ounces (227 g) peanut butter chips
- 2 pounds (907 g) lightly salted or unsalted peanuts

1. Begin by spraying the inside of the crock pot with nonstick cooking spray to prevent sticking. 2. Layer the ingredients in the crock pot according to the specified order. 3. Cover the pot and cook on low for 2 hours, avoiding the temptation to stir or lift the lid during this time. 4. After the cooking time is complete, mix the ingredients thoroughly. 5. Using a teaspoon, drop spoonfuls of the mixture onto waxed paper. Refrigerate for about 45 minutes before serving or storing. Enjoy your treats!

Maytag Blue and Walnut Dip with Apple Dippers

Prep time: 10 minutes | Cook time: 2 to 3 hours | Serves 8

- 2 (8-ounce / 227-g) packages cream cheese at room temperature
- ½ cup mayonnaise
- 2 tablespoons Ruby Port
- 6 drops Tabasco sauce

- 1 cup chopped walnuts
- 2 cups crumbled Maytag blue cheese
- 4 to 6 Granny Smith Apples, cored and cut into 8 wedges each, for serving
- Crackers for serving

1. Start by coating the insert of a 1½- to 3-quart crock pot with nonstick cooking spray. In a mixing bowl, combine the cream cheese, mayonnaise, port, Tabasco sauce, walnuts, and blue cheese, stirring until the mixture is well blended. 2. Transfer the cheese mixture to the slow cooker insert. Cover the pot and cook on low for 2 to 3 hours, or until the dip is heated through and bubbly. 3. Once ready, serve the dip directly from the cooker set on warm, accompanied by apple wedges and crackers for dipping. Enjoy your delicious appetizer!

Savory Cranberry Cream Meatballs

Prep time: 15 minutes | Cook time: 2 to 6 hours | Serves 6

- 50 meatballs, about 1½ pounds (680 g)
- 1 cup brown gravy, from a jar, or made from a mix
- 1 cup whole-berry cranberry sauce

- 2 tablespoons heavy cream
- 2 teaspoons Dijon mustard

1. Put meatballs in crock pot. 2. Mix remaining ingredients in a bowl. Pour over meatballs. 3. Cover and cook on high 2 to 3 hours or on low 5 to 6 hours.

Chapter **8**

Vegetables and Sides

Chapter 8 Vegetables and Sides

Creamy Slow-Cooked Potatoes au Gratin

Prep time: 10 minutes | Cook time: 6 to 8 hours | Serves 6

- ½ cup skim milk
- 1 (10¾-ounce / 305-g) can light condensed Cheddar cheese soup
- 1 (8-ounce / 227-g) package fat-free cream cheese, softened
- 1 clove garlic, minced
- ¼ teaspoon ground nutmeg
- ¼ teaspoon black pepper
- 2 pounds (907 g) baking potatoes, cut into ¼-inch-thick slices
- 1 small onion, thinly sliced
- Paprika
- Nonfat cooking spray

1. Heat milk in small saucepan over medium heat until small bubbles form around edge of pan. Remove from heat. 2. Add soup, cream cheese, garlic, nutmeg, and pepper to pan. Stir until smooth. 3. Spray inside of crock pot with nonfat cooking spray. Layer one-quarter of potatoes and onions on bottom of crock pot. 4. Top with one-quarter of soup mixture. Repeat layers 3 times. 5. Cover. Cook on low 6 to 8 hours, or until potatoes are tender and most of liquid is absorbed. 6. Sprinkle with paprika before serving.

Mom's Buttered and Parsleyed Potatoes

Prep time: 15 minutes | Cook time: 4 to 5 hours | Serves 6

- 2½ pounds (1.1 kg) fingerling potatoes, scrubbed and cut in half
- ½ cup (1 stick) unsalted butter, melted
- ¼ cup olive oil
- 6 fresh sage leaves, finely chopped
- 1½ teaspoons salt
- ½ teaspoon freshly ground black pepper
- ¼ cup finely chopped fresh Italian parsley, for garnish
- ¼ cup freshly grated Parmesan cheese, for garnish

1. Place the potatoes in the insert of a 5- to 7-quart crock pot. Add the butter, oil, sage, salt, and pepper, then stir well to evenly coat the potatoes with the ingredients. Cover the pot and cook on low for 4 to 5 hours, or until the potatoes are tender. 2. In a small bowl, mix together the chopped parsley and cheese, then sprinkle this mixture over the cooked potatoes. 3. Serve the potatoes hot and enjoy your delicious side dish!

Cheesy Slow-Cooked Spinach Casserole

Prep time: 10 minutes | Cook time: 5 hours | Serves 8

- 3 (10-ounce / 283-g) boxes frozen spinach, thawed and drained
- 2 cups cottage cheese
- 1½ cups shredded Cheddar cheese
- 3 eggs
- ¼ cup flour
- 1 teaspoon salt
- ½ cup butter, or margarine, melted

1. Mix together all ingredients. 2. Pour into crock pot. 3. Cook on high 1 hour. Reduce heat to low and cook 4 more hours.

Cheesy Onions

Prep time: 20 minutes | Cook time: 2 to 4 hours | Serves 6 to 8

- 1½ pounds (680 g) small onions
- 4 slices bacon, cooked and crumbled
- 1 (10½-ounce / 298-g) can
- Cheddar cheese soup
- ½ cup milk
- ¼ cup grated Parmesan cheese

1. Peel the onions, keeping them whole, and place them in the crock pot. 2. In a separate bowl, mix together the remaining ingredients until well combined. 3. Pour this mixture over the onions in the crock pot and gently stir to incorporate the onions into the sauce. 4. Cover and cook on high for 2 hours or on low for 4 hours, or until the onions are fully tender. Enjoy your flavorful dish!

Green Beans with Cipollini Onions and Cremini Mushrooms

Prep time: 15 minutes | Cook time: 4 to 5 hours | Serves 6 to 8

- ½ cup (1 stick) unsalted butter, melted
- ¼ cup soy sauce
- 2 tablespoons rice wine (mirin) or dry sherry
- 2 cloves garlic, minced
- 24 cipollini onions, peeled
- 8 ounces (227 g) cremini mushrooms, quartered
- 2 pounds (907 g) green beans, ends trimmed, cut into 1-inch lengths

1. In the insert of a 5- to 7-quart crock pot, combine the butter, soy sauce, rice wine, and minced garlic, stirring to blend the ingredients well. 2. Add the remaining vegetables to the pot and toss them to coat evenly with the butter mixture. Cover the crock pot and cook on low for 4 to 5 hours, or until the beans and onions are tender. 3. Once cooked, drain the liquid from the vegetables and serve them immediately for a delicious side dish. Enjoy!

Slow-Simmered Red Wine Mushrooms

Prep time: 5 minutes | Cook time: 6 hours | Serves 4

- 1 pound (454 g) fresh mushrooms, stemmed, trimmed, and cleaned
- 4 cloves garlic, minced
- ¼ cup onion
- 1 tablespoon olive oil
- 1 cup red wine

1. Combine all ingredients in crock pot. 2. Cook on low 6 hours.

Summer Vegetable Mélange

Prep time: 15 minutes | Cook time: 6 hours | Serves 6

- ½ cup extra-virgin olive oil
- ¼ cup balsamic vinegar
- 1 tablespoon dried basil
- 1 teaspoon dried thyme
- ¼ teaspoon salt
- 2 cups cauliflower florets
- 2 zucchini, diced into 1-inch pieces
- 1 yellow bell pepper, cut into strips
- 1 cup halved button mushrooms

1. In a large bowl, whisk together the oil, vinegar, basil, thyme, and salt until the mixture is well blended. 2. Add the cauliflower, zucchini, bell pepper, and mushrooms to the bowl, tossing to coat the vegetables evenly with the dressing. 3. Transfer the coated vegetables to the insert of the crock pot. 4. Cover the pot and cook on low for 6 hours, allowing the flavors to meld and the vegetables to become tender. 5. Once cooked, serve the vegetable medley warm and enjoy!

Greek Tomato-Braised Green Beans

Prep time: 5 minutes | Cook time: 2 to 5 hours | Serves 6

- 20 ounces (567 g) whole or cut-up frozen green beans (not French cut)
- 2 cups tomato sauce
- 2 teaspoons dried onion
- flakes (optional)
- Pinch of dried marjoram or oregano
- Pinch of ground nutmeg
- Pinch of cinnamon

1. Combine all ingredients in crock pot, mixing together thoroughly. 2. Cover and cook on low 2 to 4 hours if the beans are defrosted, or 3 to 5 hours on low if the beans are frozen, or until the beans are done to your liking.

Cauliflower-Pecan Casserole

Prep time: 15 minutes | Cook time: 6 hours | Serves 6

- 1 tablespoon extra-virgin olive oil
- 2 pounds (907 g) cauliflower florets
- 10 bacon slices, cooked and chopped
- 1 cup chopped pecans
- 4 garlic cloves, sliced
- ½ teaspoon salt
- ½ teaspoon freshly ground black pepper
- 2 tablespoons freshly squeezed lemon juice
- 4 hard-boiled eggs, shredded, for garnish
- 1 scallion, white and green parts, chopped, for garnish

1. Begin by lightly greasing the insert of the crock pot with olive oil to prevent sticking. 2. In a medium bowl, combine the cauliflower, cooked bacon, chopped pecans, minced garlic, salt, and pepper, tossing them together until evenly mixed. 3. Transfer the mixture into the crock pot insert and drizzle the lemon juice over the top. 4. Cover the pot and cook on low for 6 hours, allowing the flavors to blend and the cauliflower to become tender. 5. Once done, garnish the dish with sliced hard-boiled eggs and chopped scallions before serving. Enjoy your delicious creation!

Slow-Cooker "Baked" Sweet Potatoes

Prep time: 10 minutes | Cook time: 4 to 8 hours | Serves 6 to 8

◆ 6 to 8 medium sweet potatoes	◆ Salt to taste
	◆ Butter, for serving

1. Scrub and prick sweet potatoes with fork. Wrap each in tin foil and arrange in crock pot. 2. Cover. Cook on low 6 to 8 hours, or on high 4 to 5 hours, or until each potato is soft. 3. Remove from foil and serve with butter and salt.

Barley-Stuffed Cabbage Rolls with Pine Nuts and Currants

Prep time: 20 minutes | Cook time: 6 to 8 hours | Serves 4

◆ 1 large head green cabbage, cored	◆ 2 tablespoons chopped fresh flat-leaf parsley
◆ 1 tablespoon olive oil	◆ ½ teaspoon sea salt
◆ 1 large yellow onion, chopped	◆ ½ teaspoon black pepper
◆ 3 cups cooked pearl barley	◆ ½ cup apple juice
◆ 3 ounces (85 g) feta cheese, crumbled	◆ 1 tablespoon apple cider vinegar
◆ ½ cup dried currants	◆ 1 (15-ounce / 425-g) can crushed tomatoes, with the juice
◆ 2 tablespoons pine nuts, toasted	

1. Start by steaming the whole cabbage head in a large pot over boiling water for about 8 minutes. Once done, remove it and let it cool slightly on a cutting board. 2. Carefully take off 16 leaves from the cabbage head, reserving any remaining cabbage for another recipe. Trim the raised portion of the center vein from each cabbage leaf without cutting out the vein entirely. 3. In a large nonstick skillet, heat the oil over medium heat. Add the chopped onion, cover, and cook for about 6 minutes until tender. Transfer the cooked onion to a large mixing bowl. 4. Stir in the barley, feta cheese, currants, pine nuts, and parsley into the bowl with the onions. Season the mixture with ¼ teaspoon of salt and ¼ teaspoon of pepper. 5. Lay the cabbage leaves flat on a work surface. Take one leaf and spoon approximately ⅓ cup of the barley mixture into the center. Fold the edges of the leaf over the mixture and roll it up tightly, similar to making a burrito. Repeat this process with the remaining 15 cabbage leaves and filling. 6. Arrange the prepared cabbage rolls snugly in the crock pot. 7. In a separate bowl, combine the remaining ¼ teaspoon salt, ¼ teaspoon pepper, apple juice, apple cider vinegar, and tomatoes. Pour this mixture evenly over the cabbage rolls in the crock pot. 8. Cover the crock pot and cook on high for 2 hours or on low for 6 to 8 hours. Serve the cabbage rolls hot and enjoy!

Root Vegetable Hash

Prep time: 20 minutes | Cook time: 8 hours | Serves ¾ cup

◆ 4 carrots, peeled and cut into 1-inch cubes	◆ ⅛ teaspoon freshly ground black pepper
◆ 3 large russet potatoes, peeled and cut into 1-inch cubes	◆ ½ teaspoon dried thyme leaves
◆ 1 onion, diced	◆ 1 sprig rosemary
◆ 3 garlic cloves, minced	◆ ½ cup vegetable broth
◆ ½ teaspoon salt	◆ 3 plums, cut into 1-inch pieces

1. In the crock pot, combine the chopped carrots, potatoes, onion, and minced garlic. Sprinkle the mixture with salt, pepper, and thyme, then stir well to combine. 2. Nestle the rosemary sprig among the vegetables. 3. Pour the broth over the vegetable mixture, ensuring everything is evenly coated. 4. Cover the crock pot and cook on low for 7½ hours, or until the vegetables are tender. 5. About 30 minutes before serving, stir in the plums, cover, and continue cooking on low until they are tender. 6. Once done, remove and discard the rosemary sprig before serving the dish. Enjoy your delicious vegetable medley!

Maple-Glazed Sweet Potatoes & Apples

Prep time: 15 minutes | Cook time: 6 to 8 hours | Serves 8 to 10

◆ 3 large sweet potatoes, peeled and cubed	◆ 1 teaspoon ground cinnamon
◆ 3 large tart and firm apples, peeled and sliced	◆ 4 tablespoons (½ stick) butter, melted
◆ ½ to ¾ teaspoon salt	◆ ¼ cup maple syrup
◆ ⅛ to ¼ teaspoon pepper	◆ Toasted sliced almonds or chopped pecans (optional)
◆ 1 teaspoon sage	

1. Place half the sweet potatoes in crock pot. Layer in half the apple slices. 2. Mix together seasonings. Sprinkle half over apples. 3. Mix together butter and maple syrup. Spoon half over seasonings. 4. Repeat layers. 5. Cover. Cook on low 6 to 8 hours or until potatoes are soft, stirring occasionally. 6. To add a bit of crunch, sprinkle with toasted almonds or pecans when serving. 7. Serve.

Sweet & Savory Green Beans

Prep time: 10 minutes | Cook time: 3 to 4 hours | Serves 10

- 2 quarts green beans, drained
- ⅓ cup chopped onions
- 1 (4-ounce / 113-g) can mushrooms, drained
- 2 tablespoons brown sugar
- 3 tablespoons butter
- Pepper to taste

1. Combine beans, onions, and mushrooms in crock pot. 2. Sprinkle with brown sugar. 3. Dot with butter. 4. Sprinkle with pepper. 5. Cover. Cook on high 3 to 4 hours. Stir just before serving.

Orange-Thyme Glazed Carrots

Prep time: 10 minutes | Cook time: 4 to 6 hours | Serves 6 to 8

- ½ cup (1 stick) unsalted butter, melted
- ¼ cup honey
- 1 cup orange juice
- Grated zest of 1 orange
- 1 teaspoon dried thyme
- ½ cup chicken broth
- 2 (16-ounce / 454-g) bags baby carrots

1. Begin by coating the insert of a 5- to 7-quart crock pot with nonstick cooking spray or lining it with a slow-cooker liner as per the manufacturer's instructions. 2. In the crock pot, combine all the ingredients and stir to ensure the carrots are evenly coated. Cover the pot and cook on low for 4 to 6 hours, or until the carrots are tender. 3. Once cooked, serve the carrots directly from the crock pot, keeping the setting on warm to maintain their temperature. Enjoy!

Slow-Cooked Southern Green Beans

Prep time: 10 minutes | Cook time: 6 hours | Serves 6 to 8

- 6 strips bacon, cut into 1-inch pieces; reserve some for garnish
- 2 pounds (907 g) green beans, ends snipped, cut into 1-inch pieces
- 1 medium onion, coarsely chopped
- 1½ cups chicken broth
- 4 cloves garlic, peeled
- 6 whole black peppercorns

1. Combine all the ingredients in the insert of a 5- to 7-quart crock pot. Cover and cook on low for 6 hours, until the beans are tender. 2. Drain the beans and discard the peppercorns and garlic. 3. Serve garnished with the reserved bacon.

Hearty Bean-Stuffed Peppers

Prep time: 15 minutes | Cook time: 6 hours | Serves 4

- 4 medium green, yellow, or red sweet peppers, or a mixture of colors
- 1 cup rice, cooked
- 1 (15-ounce / 425-g) can chili beans with chili gravy
- 1 cup shredded cheese, divided
- 1 (14½-ounce / 411-g) can petite diced tomatoes, with onion, celery, and green pepper

1. Wash and dry sweet peppers. Remove tops, membranes, and seeds, but keep the peppers whole. 2. In a bowl, mix together rice, beans, and half the cheese. Spoon mixture into peppers. 3. Pour tomatoes into crock pot. Place filled peppers on top, keeping them upright. Do not stack the peppers. 4. Cover and cook on high 3 hours. 5. Carefully lift peppers out of cooker and place on a serving platter. Spoon hot tomatoes over top. Sprinkle remaining cheese over peppers.

Creamed Vegetables

Prep time: 15 minutes | Cook time: 6 hours | Serves 6

- 1 tablespoon extra-virgin olive oil
- ½ head cauliflower, cut into small florets
- 2 cups green beans, cut into 2-inch pieces
- 1 cup asparagus spears, cut into 2-inch pieces
- ½ cup sour cream
- ½ cup shredded Cheddar cheese
- ½ cup shredded Swiss cheese
- 3 tablespoons butter
- ¼ cup water
- 1 teaspoon ground nutmeg
- Pinch freshly ground black pepper, for seasoning

1. Start by lightly greasing the insert of the crock pot with olive oil to prevent sticking. 2. Add the cauliflower, green beans, asparagus, sour cream, Cheddar cheese, Swiss cheese, butter, water, nutmeg, and pepper to the insert, mixing everything together well. 3. Cover the pot and cook on low for 6 hours, allowing the flavors to meld and the vegetables to become tender. 4. Once the cooking time is complete, serve the dish warm and enjoy!

Slow-Cooked Stuffed Acorn Squash

Prep time: 15 minutes | Cook time: 5 to 6 hours | Serves 4

- 2 acorn squash
- ⅔ cup cracker crumbs
- ½ cup coarsely chopped pecans
- ⅓ cup butter, melted
- 4 tablespoons brown sugar
- ½ teaspoon salt
- ¼ teaspoon ground nutmeg
- 2 tablespoons orange juice

1. Cut squash in half. Remove seeds. 2. Combine remaining ingredients. Spoon into squash halves. Place squash in crock pot. 3. Cover. Cook on low 5 to 6 hours, or until squash is tender.

Harvard Beets

Prep time: 5 minutes | Cook time: 1 hour | Serves 6

- ⅓ cup sugar
- 2 tablespoons flour
- ¼ cup beet juice or water
- ¼ cup vinegar
- 2 (16-ounce / 454-g) cans sliced beets, drained

1. In a bowl, mix together the sugar and flour. Then stir in the beet juice and vinegar until well combined. 2. Place the beets in the crock pot and pour the sugar and vinegar mixture over them, stirring to ensure the beets are thoroughly coated. 3. Cover the crock pot and cook on high for 1 hour. After that, turn the setting to low and keep warm until you're ready to serve. Enjoy!

Maple Chipotle Sweet Potato Wedges

Prep time: 15 minutes | Cook time: 4 hours | Serves 6 to 8

- 8 medium sweet potatoes, peeled, halved lengthwise, and cut into wedges
- 2 tablespoons unsalted butter, melted
- 2 tablespoons canola oil
- 4 chipotle chiles in adobo, minced
- ¼ cup maple syrup

1. Coat the insert of a 5- to 7-quart crock pot with nonstick cooking spray or line it with a slow-cooker liner according to the manufacturer's directions. 2. Arrange the sweet potatoes in the crock pot. Combine the remaining ingredients in a small bowl, pour over the potatoes, and stir to coat the wedges. Cover and cook on

high for 4 hours, until the wedges are tender when pierced with the tip of a paring knife. 3. Serve the potatoes from the cooker set on warm.

Sweet Potato Gratin

Prep time: 15 minutes | Cook time: 4 hours | Serves 12

- 1 tablespoon butter, at room temperature
- 1 large sweet onion, such as Vidalia, thinly sliced
- 2 pounds (907 g) sweet potatoes, peeled and thinly sliced
- 1 tablespoon all-purpose flour
- 1 teaspoon chopped fresh thyme
- ½ teaspoon sea salt
- ½ teaspoon black pepper
- 2 ounces (57 g) grated fresh Parmesan cheese
- Nonstick cooking oil spray
- ½ cup vegetable stock

1. In a medium nonstick skillet, melt the butter over medium heat. Add the diced onion and sauté for about 5 minutes, or until it is lightly browned. Once done, transfer the onion to a large bowl. 2. In the same bowl, add the sweet potatoes, flour, thyme, salt, pepper, and half of the grated Parmesan cheese. Toss gently to ensure the sweet potato slices are well coated with the flour mixture. 3. Spray the crock pot with cooking oil spray to prevent sticking, then transfer the sweet potato mixture into the crock pot. 4. Pour the stock over the sweet potato mixture and sprinkle the remaining Parmesan cheese on top. Cover the crock pot and cook on low for 4 hours, or until the potatoes are tender. Serve hot and enjoy your dish!

Sherried Creamed Pearl Onions & Mushrooms

Prep time: 10 minutes | Cook time: 4 to 5 hours | Serves 8

- ½ cup (1 stick) unsalted butter, melted
- ½ cup double-strength chicken broth
- 1½ teaspoons salt
- 1 teaspoon freshly ground black pepper
- ⅛ teaspoon freshly grated nutmeg
- 1 pound (454 g) pearl onions, peeled
- 1 pound (454 g) cremini mushrooms, sliced

1. Combine all the ingredients in the insert of a 5- to 7-quart crock pot. Cover and cook on low for 4 to 5 hours, until the onions are tender and ready to serve.

Bavarian Cabbage

Prep time: 10 minutes | Cook time: 3 to 8 hours | Serves 4 to 8

- 1 small head red cabbage, sliced
- 1 medium onion, chopped
- 3 tart apples, cored and quartered
- 2 teaspoons salt
- 1 cup hot water
- 2 tablespoons sugar
- ⅓ cup vinegar
- 3 tablespoons bacon drippings

1. In the crock pot, add all the ingredients in the order they are listed. 2. Cover the pot and cook on low for 8 hours, or on high for 3 hours. 3. Before serving, stir the mixture well to combine all the flavors. Enjoy your meal!

Dill Butter Corn & Squash Medley

Prep time: 10 minutes | Cook time: 1½ to 2 hours | Serves 6 to 8

- ½ cup (1 stick) unsalted butter, melted
- 1 teaspoon salt
- ½ teaspoon freshly ground black pepper
- 2 tablespoons finely chopped
- fresh dill
- 6 cups fresh corn kernels (6 to 8 medium ears)
- 2 cups cherry tomatoes
- 4 yellow squash, cut into ½-inch pieces

1. Combine all the ingredients in the insert of a 5- to 7-quart crock pot. Cover and cook on high for 1½ to 2 hours, until the corn and tomatoes are tender. 2. Serve from the crock pot set on warm.

Zippy Vegetable Medley

Prep time: 15 minutes | Cook time: 2½ hours | Serves 4 to 5

- 1 (16-ounce / 454-g) package frozen broccoli, cauliflower, and carrots
- 1 (16-ounce / 454-g) package
- frozen corn
- 2 (10½-ounce / 298-g) cans fiesta nacho cheese soup
- ½ cup milk

1. In the crock pot, combine the broccoli mixture and corn. 2. In a microwave-safe bowl, mix the soups and milk, then microwave on high for 1 minute, or just long enough to blend the ingredients well. Once mixed, pour the soup mixture over the vegetables in the crock pot. 3. Cover the crock pot and cook on high for 2½ hours, or until the dish is hot and bubbly and the vegetables are cooked to your desired tenderness. Enjoy your delicious meal!

Savory Herb Crock Pot Stuffing

Prep time: 25 minutes | Cook time: 4 to 5 hours | Serves 8

- 3 tablespoons butter
- 3 onions, chopped
- 4 celery ribs, chopped
- ½ cup chopped fresh parsley
- 1 tablespoon chopped fresh rosemary
- 1 tablespoon chopped fresh thyme
- 1 tablespoon chopped fresh
- marjoram
- 1 tablespoon chopped fresh sage
- 1 teaspoon salt
- ½ teaspoon freshly-ground black pepper
- 1 loaf stale low-fat sourdough bread, cut in 1-inch cubes
- 2 cups fat-free chicken broth

1. Sauté onions and celery in butter in skillet until transparent. Remove from heat and stir in fresh herbs and seasonings. 2. Place bread cubes in large bowl. Add onion/herb mixture. Add enough broth to moisten. Mix well but gently. Turn into greased crock pot. 3. Cover. Cook on high 1 hour. Reduce heat to low and continue cooking 3 to 4 hours.

German Potato Salad with Sausage

Prep time: 20 minutes | Cook time: 4 to 5 hours | Serves 8

- 6 to 8 medium (3-inch) Yukon Gold potatoes, scrubbed and cut into ¼-inch thick slices
- 1 medium red onion, coarsely chopped
- 2 stalks celery, coarsely chopped
- ½ pound (227 g) kielbasa or other smoked sausage, cut
- into ½-inch dice
- ⅓ cup rice vinegar
- ¼ cup Dijon mustard
- 2 tablespoons olive oil
- 3 tablespoons light brown sugar
- ½ teaspoon mustard seeds
- ½ teaspoon celery seeds
- ½ cup finely chopped fresh Italian parsley

1. In the insert of a 5- to 7-quart crock pot, combine the potatoes, onion, celery, and sausage. In a separate mixing bowl, whisk together the vinegar, mustard, oil, sugar, mustard seeds, and celery seeds until well blended. 2. Pour the mixture over the potatoes and toss everything together to combine. Cover the crock pot and cook on low for 4 to 5 hours, or until the potatoes are tender. 3. Once cooked, remove the cover and sprinkle the dish with fresh parsley. Reduce the temperature to warm and serve directly from the cooker. Enjoy!

Special Green Beans

Prep time: 30 minutes | Cook time: 1 to 2 hours | Serves 12 to 14

- 4 (14½-ounce / 411-g) cans green beans, drained
- 1 (10¾-ounce / 305-g) can cream of mushroom soup
- 1 (14½-ounce / 411-g) can
- chicken broth
- 1 cup tater tots
- 1 (3-ounce / 85-g) can French-fried onion rings

1. Place the green beans in the crock pot. 2. In a separate bowl, mix together the soup and broth until well combined, then spread this mixture evenly over the green beans. 3. Spoon the tater tots over the top of the soup mixture, and then add the onion rings on top. 4. Cover the crock pot and cook on high for 1 to 2 hours, or until everything is heated through and the tater tots are cooked. Enjoy your hearty dish!

Onion Potatoes

Prep time: 20 minutes | Cook time: 5 to 6 hours | Serves 6

- 6 medium potatoes, diced
- ⅓ cup olive oil
- 1 envelope dry onion soup mix

1. In a plastic bag, combine the potatoes and olive oil, then shake well to coat the potatoes evenly. 2. Add the onion soup mix to the bag and shake again until the potatoes are thoroughly coated. 3. Pour the potato mixture into the crock pot. 4. Cover the pot and cook on low for 5 to 6 hours, allowing the flavors to meld and the potatoes to become tender. Enjoy your flavorful dish!

Crispy Pancetta Brussels Sprouts

Prep time: 10 minutes | Cook time: 1½ hours | Serves 6

- ½ cup extra-virgin olive oil
- 3 ounces (85 g) pancetta, finely chopped
- 3 cloves garlic, sliced
- 2 pounds (907 g) Brussels
- sprouts, ends trimmed, cut into quarters, and leaves separated
- 1½ teaspoons salt
- ½ teaspoon freshly ground black pepper

1. Heat the oil in a medium sauté pan over high heat. Add the pancetta and cook until crispy. Remove it to paper towels to drain. Add the garlic to the pan and cook over low heat until it begins to turn golden, being careful not to let it get brown. 2. Pour the oil and garlic into the insert of a 5- to 7-quart crock pot. Stir in the sprouts, salt, and pepper. cover and cook on high for 1 hour, until the leaves are tender. Stir in the pancetta and cook for another 30 minutes. 3. Serve hot or at room temperature.

North African Vegetable Stew

Prep time: 15 minutes | Cook time: 7 to 8 hours | Serves 6

- 1 tablespoon extra-virgin olive oil
- 2 cups diced pumpkin
- 2 cups chopped cauliflower
- 1 red bell pepper, diced
- ½ sweet onion, diced
- 2 teaspoons minced garlic
- 2 cups coconut milk
- 2 tablespoons natural peanut butter
- 1 tablespoon ground cumin
- 1 teaspoon ground coriander
- ¼ cup chopped cilantro, for garnish

1. Begin by lightly greasing the insert of the crock pot with olive oil to prevent sticking. 2. Add the pumpkin, cauliflower, bell pepper, onion, and garlic to the insert. 3. In a small bowl, whisk together the coconut milk, peanut butter, cumin, and coriander until the mixture is smooth and well combined. 4. Pour the coconut milk mixture over the vegetables in the crock pot, ensuring everything is evenly coated. 5. Cover the pot and cook on low for 7 to 8 hours, allowing the flavors to meld and the vegetables to become tender. 6. When ready to serve, top the dish with fresh cilantro for a burst of flavor and garnish. Enjoy your meal!

Creamy Garlic Mashed Sweet Potatoes

Prep time: 20 minutes | Cook time: 8 hours | Serves 1 cup

- Nonstick cooking spray
- 4 large sweet potatoes, peeled and cubed
- 1 onion, chopped
- 6 garlic cloves, peeled
- ½ cup orange juice
- 2 tablespoons honey
- 1 teaspoon salt
- ⅛ teaspoon freshly ground black pepper
- ⅓ cup butter, at room temperature
- ½ cup heavy cream

1. Spray the crock pot with the nonstick cooking spray. 2. In the crock pot, combine the sweet potatoes, onion, and garlic. 3. Pour the orange juice and honey over everything, and stir. Sprinkle with the salt and pepper. 4. Cover and cook on low for 8 hours, or until the potatoes are tender. 5. Add the butter and cream, mash using a potato masher or immersion blender, and serve.

Savory Green Beans with Bacon & Tomatoes

Prep time: 15 minutes | Cook time: 4½ hours | Serves 12

- 1 (14-ounce / 397-g) package thick-sliced bacon strips, chopped
- 1 large red onion, chopped
- 2 (16-ounce / 454-g) packages frozen cut green beans
- 1 (28-ounce / 794-g) can
- petite diced tomatoes, undrained
- ¼ cup packed brown sugar
- 1 tablespoon seasoned pepper
- ½ teaspoon seasoned salt
- 1 (16-ounce / 454-g) can red beans, rinsed and drained

1. In a large skillet, cook bacon over medium heat until partially cooked but not crisp, stirring occasionally. Remove with a slotted spoon; drain on paper towels. Discard drippings, reserving 2 tablespoons. Add onion to drippings; cook and stir over medium-high heat until tender. 2. In a 4- or 5-quart crock pot, combine green beans, tomatoes, brown sugar, pepper, salt, bacon and onion. Cook, covered, on low 4 hours. Stir in red beans. Cook 30 minutes longer or until heated through.

Zesty Lemon Chive Red Potatoes

Prep time: 10 minutes | Cook time: 2½ to 3 hours | Serves 6

- 1½ pounds (680 g) medium red potatoes
- ¼ cup water
- 2 tablespoons butter, melted
- 1 tablespoon lemon juice
- 3 tablespoons fresh chives, snipped
- Chopped fresh parsley
- 1 teaspoon salt
- ½ teaspoon black pepper

1. Cut a strip of peel from around the middle of each potato. Place potatoes and water in crock pot. 2. Cover. Cook on high 2½ to 3 hours. 3. Drain. 4. Combine butter, lemon juice, chives, and parsley. Pour over potatoes. Toss to coat. 5. Season with salt and pepper.

"Stir-Fry" Veggies

Prep time: 20 minutes | Cook time: 8 to 10 hours | Serves 8

- 1 (16-ounce / 454-g) bag baby carrots
- 4 ribs celery, chunked
- 1 medium onion, diced
- 1 (14½-ounce / 411-g) can low-sodium Italian-style stewed tomatoes
- ½ teaspoon dried basil
- ½ teaspoon dried oregano
- ½ teaspoon salt
- 1 large red or yellow bell pepper, diced
- 1 small head cabbage, cut up
- 1 pound (454 g) raw broccoli, cut up

1. In the crock pot, combine the carrots, celery, onion, tomatoes, basil, oregano, and salt. 2. Cover the pot and cook on high for 3 to 4 hours, or on low for 6 to 8 hours, stirring occasionally to ensure even cooking. 3. After the initial cooking time, stir in the pepper, cabbage, and broccoli. 4. Cook for an additional hour on high or 2 more hours on low, stirring occasionally. If the vegetables seem dry, add a little water to keep them moist. Enjoy your flavorful vegetable dish!

Uptown Scalloped Potatoes

Prep time: 15 minutes | Cook time: 6 to 7 hours | Serves 8 to 10

- 5 pounds (2.3 kg) red potatoes, peeled and sliced
- 2 cups water
- 1 teaspoon cream of tartar
- ¼ pound (113 g) bacon, cut
- in 1-inch squares, browned until crisp, and drained
- Dash of salt
- ½ pint whipping cream
- 1 pint half-and-half

1. Toss the potatoes in water mixed with cream of tartar, then drain well. 2. In a large crock pot, layer the potatoes and bacon, then sprinkle with salt to season. 3. In a separate bowl, mix together the whipping cream and half-and-half until well combined. 4. Pour the cream mixture over the layered potatoes and bacon. Cover the crock pot and cook on low for 6 to 7 hours, allowing the flavors to meld and the potatoes to become tender. Enjoy your delicious dish!

Cheesy Broccoli Egg Casserole

Prep time: 10 minutes | Cook time: 3 to 5 hours | Serves 6

- 1 (10-ounce / 283-g) package frozen chopped broccoli
- 6 eggs, beaten
- (24-ounce / 680-g) carton fat-free small-curd cottage cheese
- 6 tablespoons flour
- 8 ounces (227 g) fat-free mild cheese of your choice, diced
- 2 green onions, chopped
- ½ teaspoon salt

1. Place frozen broccoli in colander. Run cold water over it until it thaws. Separate into pieces. Drain well. 2. Combine remaining ingredients in large bowl and mix until well blended. Stir in broccoli. Pour into crock pot sprayed with fat-free cooking spray. 3. Cover. Cook on high 1 hour. Stir well, then resume cooking on low 2 to 4 hours.

Sweet Potato Casserole

Prep time: 10 minutes | Cook time: 3 to 4 hours | Serves 8

- 2 (29-ounce / 822-g) cans sweet potatoes, drained and mashed
- 2 tablespoons brown sugar
- 1 tablespoon orange juice
- 2 eggs, beaten
- ½ cup fat-free milk
- ⅓ cup chopped pecans
- ⅓ cup brown sugar
- 2 tablespoons flour
- 2 teaspoons butter, melted

1. In a mixing bowl, combine the sweet potatoes with 2 tablespoons of brown sugar, stirring until well mixed. 2. Add the orange juice, eggs, and milk to the sweet potato mixture, and stir until fully combined. Transfer this mixture to a greased crock pot. 3. In another bowl, mix together the pecans, ⅓ cup of brown sugar, flour, and butter until crumbly. Spread this topping evenly over the sweet potatoes in the crock pot. 4. Cover the pot and cook on high for 3 to 4 hours, allowing the dish to become warm and flavorful. Enjoy your delicious sweet potato casserole!

Slow-Cooked Herbed Cherry Tomatoes

Prep time: 10 minutes | Cook time: 1½ to 3 hours | Serves 6

- ½ cup extra-virgin olive oil
- 6 cloves garlic, sliced
- 2 teaspoons dried tarragon
- 1 teaspoon dried chervil
- ½ teaspoon dried dill
- 6 cups varicolored cherry or pear tomatoes

1. Combine all the ingredients in the insert of a 5- to 7-quart crock pot. Cover and cook on high for 1½ hours or on low for 3 hours. 2. Serve the tomatoes at room temperature.

Chapter 9

Desserts

Chapter 9 Desserts

Creamy Almond Rice Porridge

Prep time: 10 minutes | Cook time: 6 hours | Serves 6 to 8

⅓ cup basmati rice	strands (optional)
⅓ cup almonds	6 green cardamom pods, seeds only, pounded to a fine powder
4 cups whole milk, divided	
¾ cup sugar	Handful of crushed unsalted pistachios, for garnish
Generous pinch saffron	

1. Wash the rice and soak it in water for 30 minutes. 2. In a blender, grind the rice and almonds with about ⅔ cup of the milk to a coarse paste. 3. Add the remaining milk and blend to a smooth paste. 4. Pour the mixture into your crock pot. Cover and cook on high for 4 hours. 5. Add the sugar, saffron (if using), and pounded cardamom seeds. Cover and cook on low for 2 more hours. 6. Transfer into individual ceramic dishes or a large clay or earthenware pot, and leave to cool for 4 to 5 hours. 7. Garnish with pistachios and serve chilled.

Decadent Hot Fudge Pudding Cake

Prep time: 20 minutes | Cook time: 2 hours | Serves 4 to 6

½ cup milk	powder and not Dutch process)
3 tablespoons unsalted butter, melted	2 teaspoons baking powder
1 teaspoon vanilla bean paste	¾ cup firmly packed light brown sugar
1 cup granulated sugar	1¼ cups boiling water
1 cup all-purpose flour	Vanilla ice cream or unsweetened whipped cream for serving
½ cup cocoa powder (make sure to use natural cocoa	

1. Coat the insert of a 5- to 7-quart crock pot with nonstick cooking spray. Stir together the milk, butter, and vanilla bean paste in a mixing bowl. Gradually stir in the granulated sugar, flour, ¼ cup of the cocoa powder, and the baking powder. Spread the batter in the prepared slow-cooker insert. 2. Mix together the brown sugar and remaining ¼ cup cocoa powder in a small bowl and sprinkle evenly over the batter. Pour in the boiling water (do not stir). Cover and cook on high for 2 hours, until a skewer inserted into the center comes out clean. Uncover and allow to cool for about 20 minutes. 3. Serve in bowls with vanilla ice cream.

Creamy Crock Pot Cheesecake

Prep time: 25 minutes | Cook time: 2 hours | Serves 6

Nonstick cooking spray

Crust:

¾ cup graham cracker crumbs	butter, melted
	2 tablespoons sugar
2 tablespoons unsalted	

Filling:

16 ounces (454 g) cream cheese, softened	2 teaspoon vanilla extract
	2 large eggs, room temperature
½ cup sugar	
2 tablespoons all-purpose flour	½ cup plain yogurt or sour cream

1. Lightly coat a 6-inch springform pan with cooking spray; line bottom with parchment and lightly spray. Fill a 5- to 6-quart crock pot with ½ inch hot water. Set three 1-inch balls of foil in center of crock pot. Wrap slow-cooker lid tightly with a clean kitchen towel, gathering ends at top (to absorb condensation). Make the Crust: 2. Combine crumbs, butter, and sugar. Press mixture evenly on bottom and about 1 inch up sides of springform pan. Make the Filling: 3. In a food processor, pulse cream cheese, sugar, flour, and vanilla until smooth. Add eggs and process until combined. Add yogurt and process until smooth, scraping down sides of bowl. Pour filling into pan. Gently tap pan on work surface to remove air bubbles. 4. Set pan on aluminum balls in crock pot. Cover and cook on high until set and an instant-read thermometer inserted in center registers 155ºF (68ºC), 1½ to 2 hours (do not cook on low). Turn off crock pot and let cake rest, covered, 1 hour. 5. Carefully transfer pan to a wire rack to cool completely, then refrigerate until chilled, at least 4 hours and preferably overnight. Carefully remove outer ring from pan and transfer cake to a plate (remove parchment). Use a warm knife to cut into wedges, wiping blade after each cut.

Steamed Cranberry Pudding with Butter Sauce

Prep time: 20 minutes | Cook time: 3 to 4 hours | Serves 8 to 10

Pudding:
- 1⅓ cups flour
- ½ teaspoon salt
- 2 teaspoons baking soda
- ⅓ cup boiling water

- ½ cup dark molasses
- 2 cups whole cranberries
- ½ cup chopped nuts
- ½ cup water

Butter Sauce:
- 1 cup confectioners sugar
- ½ cup heavy cream or evaporated milk

- ½ cup butter
- 1 teaspoon vanilla

1. Mix together flour and salt. 2. Dissolve soda in boiling water. Add to flour and salt. 3. Stir in molasses. Blend well. 4. Fold in cranberries and nuts. 5. Pour into well greased and floured bread or cake pan that will sit in your cooker. Cover with greased foil. 6. Pour ½ cup water into cooker. Place foil-covered pan in cooker. Cover with cooker lid and steam on high 3 to 4 hours, or until pudding tests done with a wooden pick. 7. Remove pan and uncover. Let stand 5 minutes, then unmold. 8. To make butter sauce, mix together all ingredients in saucepan. Cook, stirring over medium heat until sugar dissolves.

Pakistani Sweet Rice Scented with Cardamom

Prep time: 10 minutes | Cook time: 2¼ hours | Serves 6 to 8

- 2 cups basmati rice
- 4 tablespoons butter or ghee
- 4 cups hot water
- 1 large pinch saffron, crushed and mixed with 2 tablespoons hot water, or a yellow food coloring

- 6 green cardamom pods
- ¾ to 1 cup sugar
- 2 tablespoons crushed unsalted pistachios
- 2 tablespoons slivered almonds

1. Rinse the rice in several changes of water until it runs clear, then soak it in warm water for 10 minutes. 2. Lightly grease the inside of the crock pot with a bit of butter or ghee and set it to high. Drain the soaked rice and place it in the crock pot. Add the hot water along with the saffron water (or food coloring), stirring to mix well. This will give the rice its characteristic bright yellow color. 3. Cover the crock pot and cook for 2 hours on high, stirring the rice halfway through the cooking time. Once cooked, remove the rice and set it aside in a colander to drain. 4. With the crock pot still on high, add the remaining butter to melt, then add the cardamom pods. Stir in

the sugar and 4 tablespoons of water (adding a bit more if needed), mixing until the sugar dissolves. 5. Allow the mixture to cook gently for about 5 minutes to create a syrup, then stir in most of the nuts, reserving some for garnish. 6. Gently fold the cooked rice back into the syrup mixture, ensuring that each grain is coated. 7. Cover the crock pot and turn it to low, cooking for an additional 5 to 10 minutes to allow the flavors to meld. 8. Serve the dish warm, garnished with the reserved nuts on top. Enjoy your flavorful rice!

Apple Appeal

Prep time: 10 minutes | Cook time: 4 to 5 hours | Serves 6

- 6 baking apples, peeled, cored, and quartered
- ¼ teaspoon nutmeg
- 2 tablespoons sugar

- ¾ teaspoon Asian five-spice powder
- ¼ cup apple juice

1. Place the prepared apples into the crock pot. 2. In a small mixing bowl, combine all the remaining ingredients until well mixed. 3. Pour this mixture over the apples in the crock pot, stirring gently to coat the apples evenly. 4. Cover the pot and cook on low for 4 to 5 hours, or until the apples reach your desired tenderness. 5. Serve the apples either sliced or mashed, warm, cold, or at room temperature. Enjoy your delicious apple dish!

Apple Cobbler

Prep time: 20 minutes | Cook time: 4 hours | Serves 2

- Nonstick cooking spray
- 3 apples, peeled and sliced
- 1 tablespoon freshly squeezed lemon juice
- ½ cup dried cranberries
- ½ cup chopped walnuts
- ¼ cup granulated sugar, plus

- cup, divided
- ⅔ cup all-purpose flour
- ½ teaspoon baking powder
- 1 egg, beaten
- ⅔ cup milk
- 1 teaspoon vanilla

1. Start by spraying the interior of the crock pot with nonstick cooking spray to prevent sticking. 2. Place the apples in the crock pot and sprinkle them with lemon juice, tossing to coat. Then add the cranberries and walnuts, followed by ¼ cup of granulated sugar, and toss everything together again. 3. In a medium bowl, mix the flour, the remaining ⅓ cup of granulated sugar, baking powder, egg, milk, and vanilla until the mixture is smooth. Spoon this batter evenly over the apple mixture in the crock pot. 4. Cover the crock pot and cook on low for 4 hours, or until the topping is set and cooked through. 5. Once done, serve the dish warm, accompanied by cream or ice cream for a delightful dessert!

Crock Pot Apple-Cranberry Crisp

Prep time: 20 minutes | Cook time: 4 hours | Serves 6 to 8

Filling:

- 3 pounds (1.4 kg) Granny Smith apples, peeled, cored, and cut into ¾-inch pieces
- 1 cup fresh or frozen cranberries

Topping:

- 1 cup all-purpose flour
- 2 teaspoon ground cinnamon
- 2 teaspoon coarse salt
- ¼ cup packed light brown sugar
- 2 tablespoons granulated sugar

- ¾ cup granulated sugar
- 1 tablespoon cornstarch
- 2 tablespoons unsalted butter, cut into small cubes

- 6 tablespoons cold unsalted butter, cut into small cubes
- 1 cup old-fashioned rolled oats (not quick-cooking)
- ¼ cup finely chopped pecans
- Ice cream, for serving

Make the Filling: 1. Combine apples, cranberries, sugar, cornstarch, and butter in a 5- to 6-quart crock pot; let sit 10 minutes. Stir to mix, and then press into an even layer in crock pot. Make the Topping: 2. Combine flour, cinnamon, salt, and both sugars. Cut in butter with a pastry blender, working mixture until it resembles coarse meal. Add oats and pecans, and press into small clumps. 3. Scatter topping over filling in cooker. Wrap slow-cooker lid tightly with a clean kitchen towel, gathering the ends at top (to absorb condensation). Cover, leaving lid slightly ajar so steam can escape, and cook on high until bubbling and crisp, 4 hours (or on low for 8 hours); rotate crock pot insert 180 degrees halfway through cooking to prevent scorching. Let crisp sit uncovered at least 10 minutes before serving with ice cream.

Natillas de Avellanas

Prep time: 10 minutes | Cook time: 2 hours | Serves 4

- 12 ounces (340 g) evaporated milk
- ½ cup milk
- 1 teaspoon vanilla bean paste
- 1 egg, lightly beaten

- 2 egg yolks
- ⅓ cup sugar
- 2 ounces (57 g) blanched hazelnuts, ground
- 2 to 3 ounces (57 to 85 g) brandy

1. In a medium heavy saucepan over medium heat, combine the evaporated milk and regular milk. Bring the mixture to a simmer and cook for about 4 minutes. Remove from heat, then stir in the vanilla bean paste, mixing well with a whisk. 2. In a medium bowl, combine the egg, egg yolks, and sugar, whisking until blended. 3. Gradually add the hot milk mixture to the egg mixture, whisking vigorously to prevent the eggs from cooking. 4. Pour the egg mixture through a sieve into a medium bowl to ensure a smooth consistency. Stir in the chopped hazelnuts and brandy. 5. Place four metal canning jar bands in the bottom of the crock pot to create a rack for the ramekins. 6. Evenly ladle the egg mixture into four 8-ounce (227-g) ramekins and cover each ramekin with foil. 7. Set the ramekins on the jar bands in the crock pot, ensuring they do not touch each other or the sides. Carefully pour hot water into the crock pot until it reaches about 1 inch up the sides of the ramekins. 8. Cover the crock pot and cook on high for 1 hour and 45 minutes, or until a knife inserted into the center of the custards comes out clean. Once cooked, carefully remove the ramekins from the crock pot and let them cool on a wire rack. 9. Serve the custards warm or chilled, as desired. Enjoy!

Decadent Cherries Jubilee Lava Cake

Prep time: 20 minutes | Cook time: 2 hours | Serves 4 to 6

Cherries:

- 2 (16-ounce / 454-g) bags frozen unsweetened pitted sweet cherries, defrosted and drained

Chocolate Cake:

- ½ cup milk
- 3 tablespoons unsalted butter, melted
- 1 teaspoon vanilla bean paste
- 1 cup granulated sugar
- 1 cup all-purpose flour

- ¼ cup sugar
- 2 tablespoons cornstarch
- 2 tablespoons brandy or Grand Marnier

- ½ cup cocoa powder (make sure to use natural cocoa powder, not Dutch process)
- 2 teaspoons baking powder
- ¾ cup firmly packed light brown sugar
- 1¼ cups boiling water

1. Coat the insert for a 3½- to 4-quart crock pot with nonstick cooking spray. Add all the cherries, sugar, cornstarch, and brandy to the slow-cooker insert and stir to combine. 2. Stir together the milk, butter, and vanilla bean paste in a mixing bowl. Gradually stir in the granulated sugar, flour, ¼ cup of the cocoa powder, and the baking powder. 3. Spread the batter evenly over the cherries in the slow-cooker insert. Mix together the brown sugar and remaining ¼ cup cocoa powder in a small bowl and sprinkle evenly over the batter. Pour in the boiling water (do not stir). 4. Cover and cook on high for 2 hours, until a skewer inserted into the center comes out clean. Uncover and allow to cool for about 20 minutes. 5. Serve spooned from the crock pot, so the cherries are a surprise resting on top of the cake.

Chocolate Lava Pudding Cake

Prep time: 15 minutes | Cook time: 2 to 3 hours | Serves 8

- 1 cup dry all-purpose baking mix
- 1 cup sugar, divided
- 3 tablespoons unsweetened cocoa powder, plus ⅓ cup,
- divided
- ½ cup milk
- 1 teaspoon vanilla
- 1⅔ cups hot water
- Nonstick cooking spray

1. Spray inside of crock pot with nonstick cooking spray. 2. In a bowl, mix together baking mix, ½ cup sugar, 3 tablespoons cocoa powder, milk, and vanilla. Spoon batter evenly into crock pot. 3. In a clean bowl, mix remaining ½ cup sugar, ⅓ cup cocoa powder, and hot water together. Pour over batter in crock pot. Do not stir. 4. Cover and cook on high 2 to 3 hours, or until toothpick inserted in center of cake comes out clean.

Dried Fruit

Prep time: 5 minutes | Cook time: 4 to 8 hours | Serves 3 to 4

- 2 cups mixed dried fruit
- ¼ cup water

1. In the crock pot, place the dried fruit and add enough water to cover it. 2. Cover the pot and set it to cook on low for 4 to 8 hours, allowing the fruit to soften and absorb the flavors. 3. Once done, serve the fruit warm as a delicious and comforting treat!

Apple Dish

Prep time: 20 minutes | Cook time: 2 to 2½ hours | Makes about 7 cups

- ¾ cup sugar
- 3 tablespoons flour
- 1½ teaspoons cinnamon (optional)
- 5 large baking apples, pared,
- cored, and diced into ¾-inch pieces
- Half a stick butter, melted
- 3 tablespoons water
- Nonstick cooking spray

1. Begin by spraying the interior of the crock pot with nonstick cooking spray to prevent sticking. 2. In a large bowl, combine the sugar and flour, adding cinnamon if desired, and set the mixture aside. 3. In the crock pot, mix together the apples, butter, and water. Gently stir in the flour mixture until the apples are evenly coated. 4. Cover the crock pot and cook on high for 1½ hours, then switch to low and continue cooking for an additional 30 to 60 minutes, or until the apples are cooked to your liking. 5. Once done, serve warm and enjoy your delicious dish!

Crème Brûlée

Prep time: 15 minutes | Cook time: 2½ hours | Serves 8

- Boiling water, for crock pot
- 4 cups heavy cream
- ¾ cup granulated sugar
- 1 vanilla bean, split lengthwise and seeds scraped
- 7 large egg yolks
- ¼ teaspoon coarse salt
- ½ cup superfine sugar, for topping

1. Place a 1½-quart soufflé dish inside a 5- to 6-quart crock pot. Pour in enough boiling water to reach halfway up the sides of the soufflé dish. 2. In a saucepan, combine the cream, 6 tablespoons of granulated sugar, and the vanilla bean along with its seeds. Heat the mixture over medium heat until bubbles begin to form around the edges, which should take about 7 to 8 minutes (avoid boiling). 3. In a large bowl, whisk together the egg yolks, the remaining 6 tablespoons of granulated sugar, and the salt. Gently whisk a small amount of the warm cream mixture into the egg mixture to temper it. Then, add two more ladles of the cream mixture, one at a time, whisking to combine after each addition. Gradually whisk in the remaining cream mixture. Strain the custard through a fine sieve into a large measuring cup, discarding any solids. Pour the custard into the prepared soufflé dish. 4. Cover the crock pot and cook on high until the custard is just set, which will take about 2½ hours (or on low for 5 hours). Once done, turn off the crock pot, remove the lid, and let the custard sit until the water cools enough to remove the dish. Allow the custard to cool completely, then cover with plastic wrap and refrigerate for at least 2 hours or up to 3 days. 5. Just before serving, sprinkle superfine sugar evenly over the custard. Using a kitchen torch, carefully pass the flame in a circular motion 1 to 2 inches above the custard until the sugar bubbles and turns a lovely amber color. Serve immediately and enjoy!

Zesty Brandy-Baked Pears

Prep time: 15 minutes | Cook time: 4 to 6 hours | Serves 6

- 6 fresh pears
- ½ cup raisins
- ¼ cup brown sugar
- 1 teaspoon grated lemon peel
- ¼ cup brandy
- ½ cup sauternes wine
- ½ cup macaroon crumbs

1. Peel and core pears. Cut into thin slices. 2. Combine raisins, sugar, and lemon peel. Layer alternately with pear slices in crock pot. 3. Pour brandy and wine over top. 4. Cover. Cook on low 4 to 6 hours. 5. Spoon into serving dishes. Cool. Sprinkle with macaroons. Serve.

Tempting Lemon Custard

Prep time: 10 minutes | Cook time: 3 hours | Serves 4

- 5 egg yolks
- ¼ cup freshly squeezed lemon juice
- 1 tablespoon lemon zest
- 1 teaspoon pure vanilla extract
- ⅓ teaspoon liquid stevia
- 2 cups heavy (whipping) cream
- 1 cup whipped coconut cream

1. In a medium bowl, whisk together the egg yolks, lemon juice and zest, vanilla extract, and liquid stevia until well combined. 2. Slowly whisk in the heavy cream until the mixture is smooth, then divide it evenly among 4 (4-ounce / 113-g) ramekins. 3. Place a rack at the bottom of the crock pot insert and carefully position the ramekins on the rack. 4. Pour in enough water to the crock pot to reach halfway up the sides of the ramekins. 5. Cover the crock pot and cook on low for 3 hours, allowing the custards to set. 6. Once cooked, carefully remove the ramekins from the insert and let them cool to room temperature. 7. Chill the ramekins completely in the refrigerator before serving. When ready, top with whipped coconut cream and enjoy your delightful dessert!

Perfect Crème Brûlée

Prep time: 10 minutes | Cook time: 1½ to 2 hours | Serves 6 to 8

- 8 to 10 cups boiling water
- 3½ cups heavy cream
- ⅔ cup superfine sugar
- 10 large egg yolks
- 1 tablespoon vanilla bean paste
- ¼ cup raw sugar

1. Begin by placing a rack at the bottom of a 5- to 7-quart slow cooker insert and arranging 8 (4-ounce / 113-g) ramekins on top of the rack. 2. Carefully pour in enough boiling water to reach halfway up the sides of the ramekins, then cover the cooker and set it on high to keep the water hot. 3. In a large mixing bowl, whisk together the cream, superfine sugar, and egg yolks until well blended. Add the vanilla bean paste and whisk until fully incorporated. Pour the custard mixture into the ramekins, cover each with aluminum foil, and set them on the rack in the slow cooker. 4. Cover the slow cooker and cook on high for 1½ to 2 hours, or until the custards are set. They may jiggle slightly in the center but will firm up as they cool. Once cooked, remove the lid and allow the custards to cool. Remove the foil and replace it with plastic wrap, then refrigerate until chilled. 5. Just before serving, sprinkle raw sugar evenly over each custard. Using a kitchen torch or under a preheated broiler, carefully heat the sugar until it bubbles and caramelizes. If broiling, do this in small batches to ensure even caramelization. 6. Allow the

custards to cool slightly after caramelizing the sugar, then serve and enjoy!

Wine-Poached Pears

Prep time: 15 minutes | Cook time: 2 hours | Serves 6 to 8

- 6 firm but ripe Bosc pears, stems left on, peeled
- 1 bottle Pinot Noir or other red wine
- 1 cup sugar
- 4 (1-inch) strips orange zest, removed with vegetable peeler
- 1 (3-inch) cinnamon stick, broken in half
- ½ teaspoon allspice berries

1. Preheat your 5- to 6-quart crock pot. Slice a small sliver from the bottoms of each pear so they can stand upright, then nestle the pears into the crock pot. 2. In a saucepan, combine the wine, sugar, orange zest, cinnamon stick, and allspice. Bring the mixture to a simmer, then pour it over the pears in the crock pot. Place a piece of parchment paper or cheesecloth over the fruit to keep them submerged. Cover the pot and cook on high until the pears are tender when pierced with a knife, about 2 hours (or on low for 4 hours). 3. Once cooked, carefully transfer the pears to a large bowl. Using a sieve, strain the poaching liquid over the pears and refrigerate them overnight to allow the flavors to develop. 4. The next day, pour the poaching liquid into a saucepan and bring it to a boil, reducing it until it measures about 1 cup, which should take around 10 minutes. Transfer the reduced liquid to a heatproof container and let it cool. 5. Serve the pears with the syrup drizzled over them for a delightful dessert. Enjoy!

Healthy Blueberry Pecan Crisp

Prep time: 10 minutes | Cook time: 3 to 4 hours | Serves 8

- 5 tablespoons coconut oil, melted, divided
- 4 cups blueberries
- ¾ cup plus 2 tablespoons granulated erythritol
- 1 cup ground pecans
- 1 teaspoon baking soda
- ½ teaspoon ground cinnamon
- 2 tablespoons coconut milk
- 1 egg

1. Lightly grease a 4-quart crock pot with 1 tablespoon of the coconut oil. 2. Add the blueberries and 2 tablespoons of erythritol to the insert. 3. In a large bowl, stir together the remaining ¾ cup of the erythritol, ground pecans, baking soda, and cinnamon until well mixed. 4. Add the coconut milk, egg, and remaining coconut oil, and stir until coarse crumbs form. 5. Top the contents in the insert with the pecan mixture. 6. Cover and cook on low for 3 to 4 hours. 7. Serve warm.

Brownies with Nuts

Prep time: 15 minutes | Cook time: 3 hours | Makes 24 brownies

- Half a stick butter, melted
- 1 cup chopped nuts, divided
- 1 (23-ounce / 652-g) package brownie mix

1. Begin by pouring melted butter into a baking insert designed to fit inside your crock pot. Swirl the butter around to grease the sides of the insert thoroughly. 2. Sprinkle half of the nuts over the melted butter in the insert. 3. In a mixing bowl, prepare the brownie batter according to the package directions. Spoon half of the batter into the baking insert, ensuring it covers the nuts evenly. 4. Add the remaining nuts on top of the first layer of batter, then spoon in the rest of the brownie batter over the nuts. 5. Place the baking insert into the crock pot and cover it with 8 paper towels to catch any moisture. 6. Cover the entire cooker and set it to cook on high for 3 hours. Avoid checking or removing the lid until the last hour of cooking. After 2 hours, insert a toothpick into the center of the brownies; if it comes out clean, they are done. If not, continue cooking for another 15 minutes and check again. Repeat this process until the toothpick comes out clean. 7. Once the brownies are finished cooking, carefully uncover the cooker and the baking insert, allowing the brownies to stand for 5 minutes. 8. Invert the insert onto a serving plate and use a plastic knife to cut the brownies (to prevent dragging crumbs). Serve warm and enjoy your delicious treat!

Almond Pear Crumble

Prep time: 10 minutes | Cook time: 2½ hours | Serves 8

- 1 cup firmly packed light brown sugar
- ¼ cup amaretto liqueur
- ¾ cup (1½ sticks) unsalted butter, melted
- 8 large firm pears, peeled, cored and coarsely chopped
- ½ cup granulated sugar
- ½ cup all-purpose flour
- ¾ teaspoon ground cinnamon
- ¼ teaspoon freshly grated nutmeg
- ⅔ cup sliced almonds
- Whipped cream for serving

1. Begin by coating the insert of a 5- to 7-quart crock pot with nonstick cooking spray. Add the brown sugar, amaretto, and ½ cup of melted butter to the insert, stirring until the ingredients are well blended. Place the pears in the mixture, turning them to ensure they are coated with the syrup. 2. In a small bowl, mix together the granulated sugar, flour, cinnamon, nutmeg, and almonds. Drizzle the remaining ¼ cup of melted butter into the flour mixture and stir with a fork until the mixture resembles coarse crumbs. Sprinkle

this crumb mixture evenly over the pears. 3. Cover the crock pot and cook on high for 2½ hours, or until a skewer inserted into the crumble comes out clean. Once cooked, uncover the pot and allow the crumble to cool for 30 minutes. 4. Serve the warm crumble with a dollop of whipped cream for a delicious dessert. Enjoy!

Nutty Fruit-Stuffed Baked Apples

Prep time: 25 minutes | Cook time: 1½ to 3 hours | Serves 4

- 4 large firm baking apples
- 1 tablespoon lemon juice
- ⅓ cup chopped dried apricots
- ⅓ cup chopped walnuts or pecans
- 3 tablespoons packed brown
- sugar
- ½ teaspoon cinnamon
- 2 tablespoons butter, melted
- ½ cup water or apple juice
- 4 pecan halves (optional)

1. Scoop out center of apples creating a cavity 1½ inches wide and stopping ½ inch from the bottom of each. Peel top of each apple down about 1 inch. Brush edges with lemon juice. 2. Mix together apricots, nuts, brown sugar, and cinnamon. Stir in butter. Spoon mixture evenly into apples. 3. Put ½ cup water or juice in bottom of crock pot. Put 2 apples in bottom, and 2 apples above, but not squarely on top of other apples. Cover and cook on low 1½ to 3 hours, or until tender. 4. Serve warm or at room temperature. Top each apple with a pecan half, if desired.

Lemon Poppy Seed Upside-Down Delight

Prep time: 15 minutes | Cook time: 2 to 2½ hours | Serves 8 to 10

- 1 package lemon poppy seed bread mix
- 1 egg

Sauce:
- 1 tablespoon butter
- ¾ cup water
- 8 ounces (227 g) light sour cream
- ½ cup water
- ½ cup sugar
- ¼ cup lemon juice

1. Combine first four ingredients until well moistened. Spread in lightly greased crock pot. 2. Combine sauce ingredients in small saucepan. Bring to boil. Pour boiling mixture over batter. 3. Cover. Cook on high 2 to 2½ hours. Edges will be slightly brown. Turn heat off and leave in cooker for 30 minutes with cover slightly ajar. 4. When cool enough to handle, hold a large plate over top of cooker, then invert. 5. Allow to cool before slicing.

Cinnamon-Caramel Poached Pears in Wine

Prep time: 10 minutes | Cook time: 4 to 6 hours | Serves 6

- 6 medium fresh pears with stems
- 1 cup white wine
- ½ cup sugar
- ½ cup water
- 3 tablespoons lemon juice
- 2 apple cinnamon sticks, each about 2½ to 3 inch long
- 3 whole dried cloves
- ¼ teaspoon ground nutmeg
- 6 tablespoons fat-free caramel apple dip

1. Peel pears, leaving whole with stems intact. 2. Place upright in crock pot. Shave bottom if needed to level fruit. 3. Combine wine, sugar, water, lemon juice, cinnamon, cloves, and nutmeg. Pour over pears. 4. Cook on low 4 to 6 hours, or until pears are tender. 5. Cool pears in liquid. 6. Transfer pears to individual serving dishes. Place 2 teaspoons cooking liquid in bottom of each dish. 7. Microwave caramel dip for 20 seconds and stir. Repeat until heated through. 8. Drizzle caramel over pears and serve.

Rum Raisin Arborio Pudding

Prep time: 10 minutes | Cook time: 4 hours | Serves 6

- ½ cup raisins
- ¼ cup dark rum
- 1 (12-ounce / 340-g) can evaporated milk
- 1½ cups water
- ⅓ cup granulated sugar
- ¾ cup Arborio rice
- ¼ teaspoon salt
- ¼ teaspoon ground nutmeg

1. In a small bowl, combine the raisins and rum, then cover and set aside to soak. 2. In a heavy medium saucepan, mix the evaporated milk with 1½ cups of water. Bring the mixture to a simmer over medium heat. Once simmering, add the sugar and stir until it has completely dissolved. Remove the saucepan from the heat. 3. Pour the milk mixture into the crock pot, then stir in the rice and salt until evenly distributed. 4. Cover the crock pot and cook on low for 4 hours, stirring after 1 hour and again after 3 hours. The pudding is ready when it is just set in the center. 5. Drain the soaked raisins and fold them into the pudding, along with the nutmeg. Let the pudding stand uncovered for 10 minutes. Serve warm, or chill in

the refrigerator for about 3 hours in dessert cups before serving. Enjoy your delicious rice pudding!

Mom's Old-Fashioned Rice Pudding

Prep time: 10 minutes | Cook time: 2½ to 3 hours | Serves 6 to 8

- 5 cups whole milk
- 2 cups heavy cream
- 1¼ cups sugar
- 1 teaspoon vanilla bean paste
- ½ teaspoon freshly grated
- nutmeg
- 1 cup Arborio or other medium-grain rice, rinsed several times with cold water and drained

1. Begin by coating the insert of a 5- to 7-quart crock pot with nonstick cooking spray. In a large bowl, whisk together the milk, cream, sugar, vanilla bean paste, and nutmeg until well combined. Pour this mixture into the crock pot insert, then add the rice and stir to combine everything thoroughly. 2. Cover the crock pot and cook on low for 2½ to 3 hours, or until the pudding is soft and creamy and the rice is tender. Once the cooking time is complete, remove the cover, turn off the cooker, and allow the pudding to cool for 30 minutes. 3. Serve the pudding warm, at room temperature, or chilled according to your preference. Enjoy this delightful dessert!

Five-Spice Poached Asian Pears

Prep time: 10 minutes | Cook time: 2½ hours | Serves 8

- ½ cup (1 stick) unsalted butter, melted
- 1½ cups firmly packed light brown sugar
- ½ cup dry sherry
- 1 teaspoon five-spice powder
- 1 cup pear nectar
- 8 firm pears, peeled, halved, and cored

1. Mix together the butter, sugar, sherry, five-spice powder, and pear nectar in the insert of a 5- to 7-quart crock pot. Add the pears to the slow-cooker insert and turn to coat them with the liquid. Cover and cook on high for 2½ hours until tender. 2. Remove the pears with a slotted spoon to a serving bowl and spoon the liquid from the crock pot over the pears. Serve warm or chilled.

Chunky Cranberry Apple Delight

Prep time: 15 minutes | Cook time: 3 to 4 hours | Serves 6

- 6 baking apple, peeled or unpeeled, cut into 1-inch cubes
- ½ cup apple juice
- ½ cup fresh or frozen cranberries
- ¼ cup sugar
- ¼ teaspoon ground cinnamon (optional)

1. Combine all ingredients in crock pot. 2. Cover and cook on low 3 to 4 hours, or until apples are as soft as you like them. 3. Serve warm, or refrigerate and serve chilled.

Decadent Caramel Bread Pudding

Prep time: 15 minutes | Cook time: 7 hours | Serves 2

- Nonstick cooking spray
- 6 slices French bread, cubed
- 1 cup golden raisins
- 2 eggs, beaten
- 1¼ cups whole milk
- ⅓ cup granulated sugar
- 1 teaspoon vanilla
- ½ teaspoon ground cinnamon
- ⅛ teaspoon salt
- ⅓ cup brown sugar
- 2 tablespoons butter
- 1 tablespoon water

1. Spray the crock pot with the nonstick cooking spray. 2. In the crock pot, combine the bread cubes and raisins. 3. In a medium bowl, beat the eggs, milk, sugar, vanilla, cinnamon, and salt well. Pour the egg mixture into the crock pot. 4. Cover and let stand for 10 minutes, occasionally pushing the bread down into the liquid. 5. Meanwhile, in a small saucepan over medium heat, simmer the brown sugar, butter, and water until a sauce forms, about 5 minutes. Drizzle over the bread in the crock pot. 6. Cover and cook on low for 7 hours, or until the mixture is set, and serve.

Berry-Pumpkin Compote

Prep time: 10 minutes | Cook time: 3 to 4 hours | Serves 10

- 1 tablespoon coconut oil
- 2 cups diced pumpkin
- 1 cup cranberries
- 1 cup blueberries
- ½ cup granulated erythritol
- Juice and zest of 1 orange
- ½ cup coconut milk
- 1 teaspoon ground cinnamon
- ½ teaspoon ground allspice
- ¼ teaspoon ground nutmeg
- 1 cup whipped cream

1. Begin by lightly greasing the insert of the crock pot with coconut oil to prevent sticking. 2. In the crock pot, add the pumpkin, cranberries, blueberries, erythritol, orange juice and zest, coconut milk, cinnamon, allspice, and nutmeg, mixing everything together until well combined. 3. Cover the crock pot and cook on low for 3 to 4 hours, allowing the flavors to meld and the fruit to soften. 4. Once cooked, let the compote cool for 1 hour before serving it warm, topped with a generous scoop of whipped cream. Enjoy your delicious compote!

Chapter 10

Pizzas, Wraps, and Sandwiches

Chapter 10 Pizzas, Wraps, and Sandwiches

Slow-Cooked Philly Cheese Steak Sandwiches

Prep time: 20 minutes | Cook time: 6 hours | Serves 6

- 2 medium onions, halved and sliced
- 2 medium sweet red or green peppers, halved and sliced
- 1 (1½-pound / 680-g) beef top sirloin steak, cut into thin strips
- 1 envelope onion soup mix
- 1 (14½-ounce / 411-g) can reduced-sodium beef broth
- 6 hoagie buns, split
- 12 slices provolone cheese, halved
- Pickled hot cherry peppers (optional)

1. Place onions and red peppers in a 4- or 5-quart crock pot. Add the beef, soup mix and broth. Cook, covered, on low 6 to 8 hours or until the meat is tender. 2. Arrange buns on a baking sheet, cut side up. Using tongs, place meat mixture on bun bottoms; top with cheese. 3. Broil 2 to 3 inch from heat 30 to 60 seconds or until cheese is melted and bun tops are toasted. If desired, serve with cherry peppers.

Beef Pitas

Prep time: 15 minutes | Cook time: 3 to 4 hours | Makes 2 sandwiches

- ½ pound (227 g) beef or pork, cut into small cubes
- ½ teaspoon dried oregano
- Dash of black pepper
- 1 cup chopped fresh tomatoes
- 2 tablespoons diced fresh
- green bell peppers
- ¼ cup nonfat sour cream
- 1 teaspoon red wine vinegar
- 1 teaspoon vegetable oil
- 2 large pita breads, heated and cut in half

1. Begin by placing the meat in the crock pot, then sprinkle it generously with oregano and black pepper to season. 2. Cover the crock pot and cook on low for 3 to 4 hours, until the meat is tender.

3. In a separate bowl, mix together the tomatoes, green peppers, sour cream, vinegar, and oil until well combined. 4. Once the meat is cooked, fill the pitas with the meat and top each one with the vegetable and sour cream mixture. Enjoy your delicious pitas!

Italian Sausage and Pepper Hoagies

Prep time: 15 minutes | Cook time: 6 hours | Serves 6

- 6 Italian sausage link
- 1 medium green pepper, cut into 1-inch pieces
- 1 large onion, cut into 1-inch pieces
- 1 (8-ounce / 227-g) can tomato sauce
- ⅛ teaspoon pepper
- 6 hoagie or submarine sandwich buns, split

1. In a large skillet, brown sausage links over medium heat. Cut into ½-inch slices; place in a 3-quart crock pot. Stir in the green pepper, onion, tomato sauce and pepper. 2. Cover and cook on low for 6 to 8 hours or until sausage is no longer pink and vegetables are tender. Use a slotted spoon to serve on buns.

Slow-Cooked Shredded Beef Sandwiches

Prep time: 10 minutes | Cook time: 8 to 10 hours | Makes 10 sandwiches

- 3 pounds (1.4 kg) beef chuck roast
- 1 large onion, chopped
- ¼ cup vinegar
- 1 clove garlic, minced
- 1 to 1½ teaspoons salt
- ¼ to ½ teaspoon pepper
- Hamburger buns, for serving

1. Place meat in crock pot. Top with onions. 2. Combine vinegar, garlic, salt, and pepper. Pour over meat. 3. Cover. Cook on low 8 to 10 hours. 4. Drain broth but save for dipping. 5. Shred meat. 6. Serve on hamburger buns with broth on side.

Sloppy Joes Italia

Prep time: 15 minutes | Cook time: 3 to 4 hours | Makes 12 sandwiches

- 1½ pounds (680 g) ground turkey, browned in nonstick skillet
- 1 cup chopped onions
- 2 cups low-sodium tomato sauce
- 1 cup fresh mushrooms, sliced
- 2 tablespoons Splenda
- 1 to 2 tablespoons Italian seasoning, according to your taste preference
- 12 reduced-calorie hamburger buns
- 12 slices low-fat Mozzarella cheese (optional)

1. In the crock pot, combine the ground turkey, chopped onions, tomato sauce, and mushrooms. 2. Stir in the Splenda and Italian seasoning until everything is well mixed. 3. Cover the crock pot and cook on low for 3 to 4 hours, allowing the flavors to meld and the turkey to cook through. 4. When ready to serve, spoon ¼ cup of the Sloppy Joe mixture onto each bun, adding cheese on top if desired. Enjoy your delicious Sloppy Joes!

Hawaiian Sausage Subs

Prep time: 15 minutes | Cook time: 3 hours | Serves 12

- 3 pounds (1.4 kg) smoked kielbasa or Polish sausage, cut into 3-inch pieces
- 2 (12-ounce / 340-g) bottles chili sauce
- 1 (20-ounce / 567-g) can pineapple tidbits, undrained
- ¼ cup packed brown sugar
- 12 hoagie buns, split

1. Start by placing the kielbasa in a 3-quart crock pot. 2. In a separate bowl, combine the chili sauce, pineapple, and brown sugar, mixing until well blended. Pour this mixture over the kielbasa in the crock pot. 3. Cover the crock pot and cook on low for 3 to 4 hours, or until the kielbasa is heated through and infused with the sauce. 4. Once done, serve the kielbasa on buns for a tasty meal. Enjoy!

Hearty Beef and Veggie Sloppy Joes

Prep time: 35 minutes | Cook time: 5 hours | Serves 12

- 4 medium carrots, shredded (about 3½ cups)
- 1 medium yellow summer squash, shredded (about 2 cups)
- 1 medium zucchini, shredded (about 2 cups)
- 1 medium sweet red pepper, finely chopped
- 2 medium tomatoes, seeded and chopped
- 1 small red onion, finely chopped
- ½ cup ketchup
- 3 tablespoons minced fresh basil or 3 teaspoons dried basil
- 3 tablespoons molasses
- 2 tablespoons cider vinegar
- 2 garlic cloves, minced
- ½ teaspoon salt
- ½ teaspoon pepper
- 2 pounds (907 g) lean ground beef (90% lean)
- 12 whole wheat hamburger buns, split

1. In a 5- or 6-quart crock pot, combine the first 13 ingredients. In a large skillet, cook beef over medium heat 8 to 10 minutes or until no longer pink, breaking into crumbles. Drain; transfer beef to crock pot. Stir to combine. 2. Cook, covered, on low 5 to 6 hours or until heated through and vegetables are tender. Using a slotted spoon, serve beef mixture on buns.

Savory Italian Beef Hoagies

Prep time: 15 minutes | Cook time: 8 hours | Serves 10 to 12

- 1 (3- to 4-pound / 1.4- to 1.8-kg) boneless beef chuck roast
- 3 tablespoons dried basil
- 3 tablespoons dried oregano
- 1 cup water
- 1 envelope onion soup mix
- 10 to 12 Italian rolls or sandwich buns

1. Cut roast in half; place in a 5-quart crock pot. Combine the basil, oregano and water; pour over roast. Sprinkle with soup mix. 2. Cover and cook on low for 8 to 10 hours or until meat is tender. Remove meat; shred with two forks and keep warm. Strain broth and skim fat. Serve meat on rolls; use broth for dipping if desired.

Polynesian Ham Sandwiches

Prep time: 20 minutes | Cook time: 3 hours | Serves 12

- 2 pounds (907 g) fully cooked ham, finely chopped
- 1 (20-ounce / 567-g) can crushed pineapple, undrained
- ¾ cup packed brown sugar
- ⅓ cup chopped green pepper
- ¼ cup Dijon mustard
- 1 green onion, chopped
- 1 tablespoon dried minced onion
- 12 hamburger buns or kaiser rolls, split

1. In a 3-quart crock pot, combine the first seven ingredients and mix them well. 2. Cover the crock pot and cook on low for 3 to 4 hours, or until everything is heated through. 3. Using a slotted spoon, serve ½ cup of the mixture onto each bun. Enjoy your delicious sandwiches!

Zesty French Sandwiches

Prep time: 5 minutes | Cook time: 8 hours | Makes 6 to 8 sandwiches

- 1 (4-pound / 1.8-kg) beef roast
- 1 (10½-ounce / 298-g) can beef broth
- 1 (10½-ounce / 298-g) can condensed French onion soup
- 1 (12-ounce / 340-g) bottle of beer
- 6 to 8 French rolls or baguettes

1. Begin by patting the roast dry and placing it in the crock pot. 2. In a mixing bowl, combine the beef broth, onion soup mix, and beer. Pour this mixture over the meat in the crock pot. 3. Cover the crock pot and cook on low for 8 hours, or until the meat is tender but not dry. 4. While the meat is cooking, split the rolls or baguettes and warm them in the oven or microwave until heated through. 5. Once the cooking time is up, carefully remove the meat from the cooker and let it rest for 10 minutes. Then, shred the meat with two forks or slice it diagonally into thin pieces. 6. Place the shredded or sliced meat inside the warmed rolls and serve immediately. Enjoy your delicious sandwiches!

Appendix 1: Measurement Conversion Chart

VOLUME EQUIVALENTS(DRY)

US STANDARD	METRIC (APPROXIMATE)
1/8 teaspoon	0.5 mL
1/4 teaspoon	1 mL
1/2 teaspoon	2 mL
3/4 teaspoon	4 mL
1 teaspoon	5 mL
1 tablespoon	15 mL
1/4 cup	59 mL
1/2 cup	118 mL
3/4 cup	177 mL
1 cup	235 mL
2 cups	475 mL
3 cups	700 mL
4 cups	1 L

VOLUME EQUIVALENTS(LIQUID)

US STANDARD	US STANDARD (OUNCES)	METRIC (APPROXIMATE)
2 tablespoons	1 fl.oz.	30 mL
1/4 cup	2 fl.oz.	60 mL
1/2 cup	4 fl.oz.	120 mL
1 cup	8 fl.oz.	240 mL
1 1/2 cup	12 fl.oz.	355 mL
2 cups or 1 pint	16 fl.oz.	475 mL
4 cups or 1 quart	32 fl.oz.	1 L
1 gallon	128 fl.oz.	4 L

TEMPERATURES EQUIVALENTS

FAHRENHEIT(F)	CELSIUS(C) (APPROXIMATE)
225 °F	107 °C
250 °F	120 °C
275 °F	135 °C
300 °F	150 °C
325 °F	160 °C
350 °F	180 °C
375 °F	190 °C
400 °F	205 °C
425 °F	220 °C
450 °F	235 °C
475 °F	245 °C
500 °F	260 °C

WEIGHT EQUIVALENTS

US STANDARD	METRIC (APPROXIMATE)
1 ounce	28 g
2 ounces	57 g
5 ounces	142 g
10 ounces	284 g
15 ounces	425 g
16 ounces (1 pound)	455 g
1.5 pounds	680 g
2 pounds	907 g

Appendix 2: Recipes Index

Made in the USA
Monee, IL
07 January 2025

76184474R00059